The House Of Fear Presents
GHOST STORIES, VOLUME 1

DAN BIANCHI

HOUSE OF FEAR PUBLICATIONS
New York City, New York
Houseoffearnyc@aol.com

To Cynthia

The House Of Fear Presents
GHOST STORIES, VOLUME 1
By Dan Bianchi
Copyright c. 2012

ISBN- 13: 978-0615583020
ISBN – 10: 0615583024
BISAC: Drama / Anthologies

GHOST STORIES, Volume 1

All Scripts By Dan Bianchi
Adapted From Stories By Listed Authors

Welcome to the *Theatre Of Imagination!*

The House Of Fear Presents offers easy-to-read, easy-to-produce scripts to those who want to create a unique style of theatrical presentation...and they make for fine reading, as well! Also, they contain unique content found in the genres of HORROR, WEIRD and SCIENCE FICTION.   However, these specially formatted scripts may also be produced as RECORDED WORKS, RADIO BROADCASTS...or, they may even be used as the basis for FILM and VIDEO presentations.

Though most of these scripts have been created to blend both intimate story-telling and cinematic styles requiring recorded SOUND DESIGN, MUSIC CUES and voices on MICROPHONES...in which there are no props, no sets, no costumes...some stories may be adapted to fit TRADITIONAL PLAY format.

The House Of Fear Presents stories containing characters, plots and action you won't find in traditional theatre: mad scientists, giant man eating plants, werewolves, vampires, ghosts and intergalactic invasions ....from King Kong smashing Radio City Music Hall and climbing the Empire State Building... to the battlefields of war, or, to the internal voice of a man going insane...from a poignant story of a woman waiting for her husband to die...to a screaming skull frightening the new resident of a haunted house!   Turn the lights down low and turn on your imaginations to fill in the visuals.

Many of the longer stories are classic works of world fiction: THE INVISIBLE MAN, THE WAR OF THE WORLDS, DRACULA, FRANKENSTEIN, THE TIME MACHINE, THE ISLAND OF DR.MOREAU, KING KONG...But, *The House Of Fear* prides itself on its great collection of famous short works from an earlier time by H.G.Wells, Bram Stoker, H.P.Lovecraft, Edgar Allan Poe, Ambrose Bierce, Robert E.Howard...and, not-so-famous works by long ignored giants of macabre literature, such as, Algernon Blackwood, Edith Nesbit, F.Marion

Crawford, Sheridan Le Fanu, etc.

These are tales to be told in near darkness. The scripts require not just great actors, but, great STORY TELLERS. This role is often listed in a script as NARRATOR. Sometimes, it may be left to the Director's discretion to cast the NARRATOR as either male or female. The story may also require actors to play multiple characters...or, a Director may choose to cast many actors to play these roles. Minor roles may also be recast as either sex.

All scripts are expertly crafted for presentation by DAN BIANCHI, Artistic Director and Founder of NYC's award-winning, critically acclaimed Radiotheatre. He has worked over 40 years as writer/director in stage and film media, and, to date, he's the most produced, living stage writer in NYC. In most cases, the archaic language of 19th Century works has been updated, but, Mr.Bianchi has tried to retain the literary author's original artistic intention and creation. Characters' names, locations, time frames may be changed. Plots may be condensed, endings may be modified, etc. Remember...the original story was intended to be read as literature and not intended to be presented in a different medium using 21st Century technology. In every case, it is Mr. Bianchi's primary goal to deliver a great story filled with optimal sound design as a most important part of the production.

SOUND DESIGN: Sound effects and dramatic music are an integral part of these stories, as necessary as the actors. Scripts contain some, but, not all, printed sound/music cues necessary to make easier reading. Directors may wish to add or change cues or even provide live music accompaniment. If you do NOT wish to create your own sound design, but, instead wish to purchase pre-recorded cues and music, please contact: houseoffearnyc@aol.com.

For More House Of Fear Titles: www.houseoffear.org

All scripts printed under the title THE HOUSE OF FEAR

PRESENTS are copyrighted and are protected by copyright laws and conventions.

Copyrights and Royalties

COPYING all or part of a script by any means, including mechanical, photocopying, videotaping, scanning, web posting or other digital media formats without permission is a violation of federal and international copyright law. Please purchase the correct number of scripts needed for your production. Anyone found in violation of this may be prosecuted to the full extent of the law. In addition, *The House of Fear Presents* reserves the right to assess an infringement penalty up to ten times the original cost owed for photocopying a script. If you order more than one copy of the same script title, you will be billed and obligated to pay licensing (royalty) fees unless you inform *The House Of Fear Presents* that your selections are for perusal only.

LICENSING FEES are due when a play is performed in front of any size audience when an admission fee is charged. Class room, free readings and free audience-attended rehearsals are excused. PERFORMANCE RIGHTS will be granted when licensing fees are received by *The House Of Fear Presents* no later than two weeks prior to the first performance. Violators will be prosecuted to the full extent of the law. An infringement penalty up to ten times the original cost owed will be issued against anyone producing any of the included scripts without first acquiring proper rights.

You may not edit a script without prior permission from the author. No changes, interpolations, or deletions in the text or title shall be made for the purpose of the production. Changing gender of a character or geographic locations are possible as long as it does not change the plot or intent of the author in any way. All requests for changes must be approved in writing by *The House Of Fear Presents* before a live production. Under no circumstances does making changes to the script exempt one from paying full royalties and properly crediting the author and *The House Of Fear Presents.*

Whenever a play is produced, due authorship credit must be given on all programs, printing and advertising for the play.

Any material, music or sound effects added to any script enclosed must be in the public domain, or originally produced and owned by the producing company. *The House Of Fear Presents* will not be held liable for any violation of the above.

Listed licensing fees on the script and on www.houseoffear.org are for live stage produtions by AMATEUR groups with maximum seating capabilities below 300. Special arrangements must be made by professional groups and amateur groups with larger seating capacity. Please contact our office for licensing fee quotations: houseoffearnyc@aol.com. Please include details about the planned performance (seating capacity, price per ticket, etc.) Production rights for any play listed on our website, because of circumstances beyond our control, may be withdrawn at any time without prior notice.

For BROADCAST, FILM and VIDEO rights, please contact: houseoffearnyc@aol.com

THE MEZZOTINT
By Dan Bianchi
From A Story By M.R. James

Cast – 3m
Running Time – 15 min
Synopsis – A picture in a gallery tells a gruesome tale

(MUSIC)

NARRATOR
"Last February, while I was assembling a sale at our auction house…I came across an interesting late addition, Number 978 in the catalogue. A mezzotint by an unknown artist. View of a manor-house, early 19th century, 15 by 10 inches… black frame. Starting bid, $1200. It was not especially exciting, and the price seemed high. Now, we deal with the greatest names in the history of art, but, for some reason, this little unsigned picture intrigued me. I was drawn to it. Why? It looked like countless other pictures of old, quaint manor houses you'd see on any household wall. Full on view, three rows of windows, trees on either side, a brick wall out front with crumbling vases and vines and shrubbery. Probably not a real house in an actual location. Frankly, it looked to be the work of an amateur. Who would pay $1200 for that? But…on the back…there was a piece of paper glued to it, torn, with the remaining words reading…ngley Hall …and…ssex."

JOHNSON
Half the name's gone. What do you think of it?

NARRATOR
Something-ly Hall…probably upstate…either in Sussex or Essex county, I suppose. If we had an actual location, the picture might be a bit more valuable.

JOHNSON
I know. Mr.Grayson put $1200 on this. Can you believe it? Maybe, $50.

NARRATOR
Maybe. It's only a print. It's really a wretched engraving.

JOHNSON

And, no figures in it. Buyers like to see farmers or even cows in their country scenes. $1200? I don't know. I mean...well, I suppose it's not very badly done. The moonlight...and...well, will you look at that? How did I overlook that?

NARRATOR

What?

JOHNSON

Look there. Right there on the edge in front. There is a figure!

NARRATOR

You're right! How did I not see that?

JOHNSON

Well, it's just a head, in the very front of the picture. Hardly more than a black blot, but, the head of a man... or woman, a good deal muffled up... back turned to the spectator, and looking towards the house. Amazing.

NARRATOR

Yes. Makes the picture all the more interesting now.

JOHNSON

Yes, well, now the picture's worth at least $100. If only we knew the actual location, it might be worth double that. Let's guess. If the vowel before the ng had only been left, it would have been easy enough...but as it is, the name may be anything...I've heard of a Langley Hall...but, that's much more grand than this place.

NARRATOR

You know...the more I look at it...I'm beginning to like this work. Has the feeling of the Romantic period. The lighting is...not bad. But, that figure...there's nothing much to it, yet, somehow, it's impressive.

JOHNSON

Yes. It's beginning to grow on me, too.

(MUSIC)

NARRATOR

"Well...we put the picture aside and went on about our duties preparing for the big sale. Later, in the evening, I am just about to lock up the gallery, when I thought I'd take one last look at the little mezzotint which had been lying on a table. What do I see? Well, a shock runs up my spine! I take one glance at the picture and...That's impossible! But, it's true. It's there. Right there in the middle of the lawn in front of the manor house...there is a figure where no figure had been before, I'm certain of it. And...it's crawling on all fours towards the house...it appears to be wearing a strange black garment with a white cross on the back. Now, as you can imagine, my heart is racing. I think I'm seeing things. How can it be? This isn't a figure hidden in the shadows off to the side. It's right in the middle of the picture. I don't know what to do next...so, I lock the picture in the vault for the night.

(MUSIC)

"Hours later, I return home...but, of course, I cannot get that image out of my mind. Obviously, I'm not going mad. Mr.Johnson, he saw the image himself...well, in an earlier version of it. Now, the figure...it has moved to a different position in the landscape. And tomorrow?

(MUSIC)

"The next day...I remove the picture from the vault and without even looking at it, I place it into the hands of Mr.Johnson..." There. Take a look for yourself. Do you see the figure? Right in the middle of the lawn?

JOHNSON

No. I see the house and moonlight and trees...

NARRATOR

What? Let me see...but...it was there. Right there on the lawn, crawling, with a cloak and a cross and...

JOHNSON

Well, wait...the moon...it was full before...it's now behind the clouds.

NARRATOR

You're right. It was big and full before.

JOHNSON

And, what's that?

NARRATOR

What?

JOHNSON

There, one of the windows on the ground floor...left of the door...it's open.

NARRATOR

Is it really? It is. Oh my God...he must have got in.

JOHNSON

If you say so.

NARRATOR

Something is going on here. I don't know what, but....
Look...here's what we'll do. I want you and I to write down exactly what we see here now in this picture.

JOHNSON

What *is* going on here?

NARRATOR

And we'll have it photographed. And, we have to find out what this place is. Where it is.

JOHNSON

I can photograph it. Do you think it's haunted?

NARRATOR

The picture or the place?

JOHNSON

Both!

NARRATOR

He got in. He was creeping up to the house and he got in
through the open window. But, why? For what reason?

JOHNSON

My family has property up in Sussex county. My father grew
He may be familiar with this place. I'll ask him right away. But,
first, the photograph. What are you going to do? Sit and watch
it all day?

NARRATOR

I don't know. Something tells me...it doesn't work like that.
Between the time I saw it last night and this morning, there was
time for lots of things to happen, but, the person, the figure,
whatever it is...only got into the house.
It could easily have completed its business in that time and
returned to its own place again... but, the fact of the window
being open, I think, must mean that it's in there now. So, I think
I can leave it awhile. Besides, I feel as if it won't change much
in the daytime. Let's take a photo and put it away for awhile.
We'll check it again by evening.

JOHNSON

Wait. You do realize...what we are confronted with here...well,
it's really weird, you know?

NARRATOR

All the more why we'll have to apply some scientific
research before we're certain of what we're dealing with...

JOHNSON

And, what if it has nothing to do with science?
                                        (MUSIC, CLOCK STRIKES)

NARRATOR

"Try to imagine keeping such a secret to yourself for an entire
day. I can't keep my mind on my work and we have our first
day of viewing in the gallery by only our most exclusive clients.
Naturally, they won't be interested in the lowly mezzotint. The
minor works are kept off the viewing floor. When the last of the
potential bidders leave for the night..."

JOHNSON

Well? Shall we open the vault and take a look?

NARRATOR

But, first…I want to be doubly sure that someone is not playing a trick on us. And, I want to be sure that we're not going mad.

JOHNSON

What? The both of us…at the same time?

NARRATOR

We need another witness. Someone who can give us another viewpoint. I've asked the security guard, William, to come in…Ah, there he is now…William…please, come in, come in.

WILLIAM

I hope you're not going to need my advice on one of those Rembrandts out there…not my cup of tea.

NARRATOR

Not at all, not at all. But, Mr.Johnson and I…we have another picture here. Nothing much. A simple little thing. Still, we are at odds and ends about it and we'd like a third opinion.

WILLIAM

You want *my* opinion?

JOHNSON

Why not? You're surrounded by art all day. You hear how we talk about it with the clients. Just give us your own unadulterated opinion…

NARRATOR

Actually…we need you to describe it…in your own words. I'm not even going to look at it, or influence you. I'm just taking it out of the vault here and …go on, you tell us what you see…

WILLIAM

Ah, well…alright. What I see…well, to begin with…it's not the sort of picture I'd hang in my own house where my little girl might see it.

JOHNSON

Why not?

WILLIAM

One look at that thing there, that skeleton or whatever it is...carrying off that poor baby and she'd scream her head off.

NARRATOR

Here...let me see that!

JOHNSON

Oh my God...

WILLIAM

I've never seen a picture like that in this gallery, that's for sure. Why would you want to show that to anyone? It's...

NARRATOR

Yes, thank you, William. That will be all. Thanks for all of your help.

WILLIAM

Good night.

JOHNSON

Good night. We'll lock up.

NARRATOR

I see it, but...I don't...

JOHNSON

The moon is gone...the window is shut...and the figure is on the lawn again...only this time, it isn't crawling...it's running...running toward us...

NARRATOR

The face...it can't be seen much in the shadows but...it's definitely white, roundish forehead...

JOHNSON

A skull. A skeleton as William seen it. But, look, in its arms...a child. Dead or alive...

NARRATOR
Who knows? The legs look terribly thin.

JOHNSON
What is exactly going on here? In this picture?

NARRATOR
I suppose we can come up with a dozen scenarios.

JOHNSON
Well, what do we do now? We can't just sit here and stare at it all night.

NARRATOR
No...I suppose not.   Let's close up and see what the morning brings...

(MUSIC)

"Well, as you might expect...we can hardly wait to open up the gallery the next morning, as we make our way quickly to the vault."

JOHNSON
My oh my...isn't that something?   The figure is gone ...and there's the house just sitting there quietly under the moonbeams as if nothing had happened.

NARRATOR
Did it? *Did* something happen?

JOHNSON
Look here...in the morning mail. It's from my father...ah, a guide book to Sussex...he has it marked off...well, now...

NARRATOR
What? What is it?

JOHNSON
Listen to this...(Reads) "Anningley. The church has been an interesting building of Norman date, but was extensively classicized in the last century. It contains the tombs of the family of Weatherbys, whose mansion... Anningley Hall..."

NARRATOR

Aha! Anningley Hall.

JOHNSON

"... a solid Queen Anne house, stands immediately beyond the churchyard in a park of about 80 acres. The family is now extinct, the last heir having disappeared mysteriously... in infancy... in the year 1802..."

NARRATOR

Don't stare at me like that.

JOHNSON

Gone missing...in infancy.

NARRATOR

I know, I know. Keep reading.

JOHNSON

"The father, Squire Arthur Weatherby, was locally known as a talented amateur engraver in mezzotint."

NARRATOR

Oh my God!

JOHNSON

"After his son's disappearance he lived in complete retirement at the Hall... and was found dead in his studio on the third anniversary of the disaster... having just completed an engraving of the house, impressions of which are of considerable rarity."

NARRATOR

Well, what do you know about that? But, does it say anything about the mysterious figure in the picture?

JOHNSON

My father jotted down a note to me here...he says... "I remember people would talk about the place and the legend behind it...seems the Squire Weatherby back then would enact cruel punishment upon poachers found on the estate. Well, as the story goes…one poacher, Gawdy his name was…Squire Weatherby could never quite catch him for years until one night, he had him cornered with the goods. There was no trial and jury. The Squire's men just hung him there on the spot and buried him in a big black cloak with a white cross on it…"

NARRATOR

Oh my…! (Pause) Go on…

JOHNSON

"…a big black cloak with a cross on it…I believe they did such things to pariahs or plague victims earlier on…and put him in an unmarked grave. And…here's the really cruel part…they were not just satisfied with that… they put an end to Gawdy's own little boy too…for fear that he might take revenge upon them in the future."

NARRATOR

Bastards!

JOHNSON

"Meanwhile…Squire Weatherby had only produced one male heir to the estate. And that child…was taken from his crib in the dead of night. By whom? No one knows. But, he was never seen again. The Squire died alone and the estate fell into disrepair."

NARRATOR

Is that it?

JOHNSON

That's all he's written.

(MUSIC)

NARRATOR

"I have only to add that the picture is now in the Cartwright Museum. With its strange pedigree and gruesome history attached…true or false, as it might be…it's now gained some notoriety and is extremely valuable. After we told our story…it was examined by a few specialists who then humored us with the idea that, perhaps, the ink used in the print had been some odd concoction...like invisible ink that appears under a change in temperature and so forth. Even so, I have no idea why that might have created the images we had witnessed. Of course, they've found nothing odd about it."

MORELLA
By Dan Bianchi
From A Story By Edgar Allan Poe

Cast - 1m, 1w
Length - 15 min.
Synopsis - A man marries a wicked woman who returns to him
from the dead.

(THUNDER.
RAIN. MUSIC)

NARRATOR
"How has it come to this? How? Remember! Remember!
When? Two? Three years ago? Try to recall. Yes, I
remember…attending a social gathering in town, at the
Radcliffe House. Music, dancing, drinking. I'm bored, lonely,
about to leave, when…I look up and there she is…all dressed in
black, as if, in mourning. Her eyes, those melancholy eyes,
staring deeply into mine. Strange. There is
some….force…between us. A spiritual connection. We know
right away that our spirits are bound together forever. Oh, I
don't mean we will become lovers. I am infatuated with her,
surely…she is beautiful… but, for *love* to exist, there must
be…well, in any case, we get married. Quite simply, she
swears herself to me and from that moment on, she shuns the
rest of the world. What can I say? I am a lucky man.

(MUSIC)

"Time goes on. I find Morella is not an ordinary woman. She's
talented and very intelligent. At times, I feel as if I am her pupil.
She speaks many languages. And smart?
She can easily attend Harvard or Yale. But, aside from
the basic academics…she also devotes a great deal of her time
to studying what is called… the dark arts. Mystical writings
that no university would dare teach."

MORELLA
Come, join me. I want you to read this…and this…

NARRATOR

"I cannot resist her. So, I delve into the unspeakable works laid before me. It's as if I have no thoughts of my own. I am completely under my wife's guidance. My mind, as well as, my heart and soul. And body...though it might not be considered *lovemaking*, yes, we do revel in the pleasures of the flesh."

MORELLA

Together, we will enter into another world beyond our own.

NARRATOR

"Morella just has to place her cold hand upon my own and rake up the ashes of a dead philosophy and some incantation whose strange meaning burns itself upon my memory. For hours, I listen to her voice tainted with terror...an unearthly sound... and there falls a shadow upon my soul... I grow pale. Soon, what was joy begins to fade into horror. The most beautiful becomes the most hideous. Meanwhile, Morella talks incessantly, obsessively, about her belief..."

MORELLA

Our identity...perhaps, it is not lost at the time of death forever.

NARRATOR

"What does she mean by that? Wait and see. Now... things begin to get unbearable for me. My wife's manner...oppresses me as if I've been under a spell. A curse! That's it. That's how one may describe it. I can no longer bear the touch of her thin fingers...nor the low tone of her voice...nor the dull glow of those melancholy eyes. I know, I know. Why don't I say something to her?
Let her know how I feel about all this? I do. I do ask, but, she won't discuss it. I suppose she considers me a weak man. Sometimes, she'll just shake her head and say..."

MORELLA

It all has to do with Fate...

NARRATOR

"As if she knows that some great unknown power beyond herself has caused this to happen. Anyway, months drag on... I begin to notice the blue veins in her pale forehead becoming prominent...and her cheeks are withdrawn and her eyes are glazed..."

MORELLA

I am with child.

NARRATOR

"Yes, our child. But, it's also apparent that the poor woman has little time to live. In an instant, my anger and fear melt into pity. How could I have been so damned afraid of her? Stupid, silly man. I must express my abject apologies, but, no sooner do I turn my gaze to her eyes... staring at me...it makes my blood run cold. I can't explain why, but...
(MORELLA MOANS IN PAIN)

"Shall I say that I want her dead? I do. Not because I am afraid of her, but, I do not want her to suffer. She doesn't deserve to die this way. But, she lingers on. Her fragile spirit clings to life for days, weeks, even months, until my tortured nerves control my mind. As time passes, I grow furious. I curse the days, the hours, which seem to lengthen and lengthen as her gentle life declines...like shadows in the dying of the day.
(MORELLA MOANS)

"But one autumn evening, Morella calls me to her bedside."

MORELLA

Come! Come!

NARRATOR

"She's had more than enough laudanum. I try my best to understand that whatever has happened between us... I don't want her to die like this. It's not right."

MORELLA

There is a dim mist over all the Earth and a warm glow upon the waters, and, amid the rich October leaves of the forest, a rainbow from the firmament has surely fallen.

NARRATOR

Save your breath, my darling.

MORELLA

It is a day of days, a day of all days either to live or to die. It is a fair day for the sons of Earth and life...ah, more fair for the daughters of heaven and death!

NARRATOR

"I kiss her forehead."

MORELLA

I am dying, yet shall I live.

NARRATOR

Morella!

MORELLA

The days have never loved me. But, her whom in life you did abhor, in death you shall adore.

NARRATOR

Don't say that...Morella!

MORELLA

I am dying. But within me is a pledge of that affection which you have given me. You dared to love me. I know it. And, so, when my spirit departs shall the child live... your child and mine, Morella's child. But, I also know that you hate and fear me...

NARRATOR

Why do you say that?

MORELLA

So, your days shall be days of sorrow...that sorrow which is the most lasting of impressions, as the cypress is the most enduring of trees. For the hours of your own happiness are over.

NARRATOR

Morella! Why do you say that? What have I done to...?
                    (MORELLA MOANS, SCREAMS)

"Now, the midwives enter and do their business and soon...
                    (BABY CRIES)

"After a slight tremor, Morella dies. As she had predicted, in dying she has given birth...and our daughter, I am told, did not draw her first breath until the mother had stopped breathing.

(MUSIC)

"Years whirl by. The child grows strangely in stature and intellect, and is the perfect resemblance of her dead mother. And I love her with a love more fervent than I had ever believed possible to feel for any human being. But, will it last? Not likely. You see...horror surrounds us. I told you, the child grows strangely in stature and intelligence. Strange, indeed, because her body size increases quite rapidly. And, as for her intellectual development... each day I discover the child to have the powers and faculties of an adult woman. The words that come from her mouth...the wisdom? From a child? It doesn't take long to realize that something dark and terrible is at work behind it all. And, always my thoughts return to the entombed Morella.

"And this is the way I live, terrified, year after year...day after day, gazing upon her holy, and mild, and eloquent face, and witnessing her body turn mature while discovering new points of resemblance to her mother.

They grow more definite, more perplexing, more hideously terrible. Her smile is like her mother's. I can bear that. Her eyes are like Morella's. I can endure that. But, when they look down into the depths of my soul with Morella's own intense and bewildering meaning...? Then, there is the contour of the high forehead, the ringlets of the silken hair, the thin fingers ... the deep sound of her voice and above all, oh, above all, when she speaks the same phrases and expressions...how can she know these words? Said in the same tone of voice as...well, It consumes me with horror. It's like a worm in my brain that will not die.

"In a sense, I lost two loves of my life. Do you want to know something? I've never even named my daughter. I call her simply, My Child. Morella's name died with her at her death. I've never spoken about her to our daughter. I forbid her to question me about her mother. During the brief period of her existence, my daughter has seen little of the outside world. What can I do to stop this travesty from progressing further? And it comes to me! Perhaps, if she were baptized, we may be spared the terrors of destiny. Fate! How dare Morella terrorize me with the concept of helplessness. My daughter shall be baptized.

"But, I need a name for her. I can think of many, of course. Gentle, good, happy names. I make my choice. But, what happens? When I stand at the baptismal font with the child next to me...and the priest before me, prompting me for a name...and I cannot say the name I have chosen. No! There is something gnawing at my thoughts. Some demon urging me to breathe that sound, that name, which, in its very recollection will make my blood run cold! Some fiend speaking from the recesses of my soul...and so, here, standing in the dim aisle, in the silence of the night...I answer with a whisper...Morella.

(WIND, THUNDER, GLASS CRASH,
SCREAM)

"What devil's work is this! My child convulses...her skin is turning white! Her eyes to glass...she's falling back upon the marble slab and responding..."

MORELLA (ECHO)

I am *here!*

NARRATOR

"Those few simple sounds fall coldly, distinctly, within my ear, and like molten lead, it hisses deeply into my brain. I shall never forget this moment for as long as I live.

(MUSIC)

"Unfortunately, I live a long time. In sorrow. Haunted."

MORELLA (ECHO)

Morella!

NARRATOR

"The winds breathe but one sound within my ears and the ripples upon the sea murmur evermore..."

MORELLA (ECHO)

Morella.

NARRATOR

"Today, my child has died and with my own hands I bear her to
our family mausoleum.

(IRON DOOR CREAKS OPEN)

"And when I open the tomb…and then the lid of the family
coffin where I will lay the child alongside her mother
…I…I…can't help but laugh. (Laughs Maniacally) You *see?*
It's *empty!* The coffin…all this time! It's *empty!"*

MORELLA (ECHO)

Morella. (Laughs Devilishly)

THE MONKEY'S PAW
By Dan Bianchi
From A Story By W.W.Jacobs

Cast – 3m, 1w
Running Time – 15 min
Synopsis – A mother wishes her dead son alive again

(THUNDER)

MRS WALSH
Listen to that thunder. The wind, the rain. Well, at least it's warm and cozy in here by the fire.

MR WALSH
This weather has been…well, that's the worst of living so far out here. Miles from nowhere. The path's become a bog. The road is like a river. The county doesn't do a thing. They were supposed to pave that road last Spring. I suppose they don't care about us stuck out here.

MRS WALSH
Never mind, dear. Jack McCarthy won't get here any sooner with you complaining.

MR WALSH
He's over two hours late now. Something must have happened.

MRS WALSH
There's a storm out there, remember?

MR WALSH
Listen? Is that the front gate? That must be him now.

(KNOCK)

I'll get it.

(DOOR OPEN)

Ah, Jacky boy, in the flesh…come in, lad, come in…

JACKY

Hello!

MR WALSH

Look at you! Come in, out of that hellish night! Feel like a nip of Scotch on a night like this?

JACKY

Don't mind!

MRS WALSH

I'll make tea.

MR WALSH

How long has it been, Jacky boy? Look at you! A man he's become. Two years since you and our Bobby have gone into the Army.

MRS WALSH

Have you seen him, our Bobby?

JACKY

I seen him in Paris four weeks ago.

MRS WALSH

Paris! How did he look? Is he alright?

JACKY

Sure. He's fine.

MRS WALSH

We've got no word from him in ages.

JACKY

The mail has slowed down a bit now that the war's over. There's a lot of confusion over there.

MR WALSH

When you went away, you were a slip of a youth. Now look at you. Off seeing the world in your uniform. Look at his medals, Martha. I'd love to travel, just to look around a bit.

JACKY

Better to stay where you are, Mr. Walsh, believe me. You wouldn't want to see what I've seen.

MR WALSH

I'm sure it's terrible. Terrible. Hey, one thing on my mind...What was that you wrote about...telling me about a monkey's paw or something?

JACKY

Nothing. Nothing worth hearing.

MRS WALSH

Monkey's paw?

JACKY

Well, it's just a bit of what you might call magic. Gypsy magic. I got it from a fortune teller in Paris.

MRS WALSH

I don't like magic.

JACKY

Here, see? I've got it here. A good luck charm. To look at it, it's just an ordinary little paw, dried like a mummy. Supposedly, it had a spell put on it by an old holy man. He wanted to show that fate ruled people's lives, and that those who interfered with it did so to their sorrow. He put a spell on it so that three separate men could each have three wishes from it.

MR WALSH

Three wishes. Well, why haven't you made three wishes, then?

JACKY

I have.

MRS WALSH

You did? Did you really have the three wishes granted?

MR WALSH

What did you wish for?

JACKY

I can't say.

MRS WALSH

And has anybody else wished?

JACKY

The first man who owned it...he had his three wishes.

MRS WALSH

What did he wish for?

JACKY

I don't know what his first two wishes were, but the third was for death. At least, that's what the fortune teller told me.

MRS WALSH

You mean, he wished to die? Who would wish such a thing?

JACKY

I was the second man to try his fate with the monkey's paw. As you can see, it hasn't done me any good. The legend was right. It's caused me more grief than happiness, I can tell you. Good luck charm? Ha! I don't know why I keep the cursed thing.

MR WALSH

Well, then, Billy...if you've had your three wishes it's no good to you now then. What do you keep it for?

JACKY

I don't know. I did want to sell it, but I don't think I will. It's caused enough heartache already. Besides, who would believe me? They'd think it's a fairy tale. Some have offered to try it first and pay me afterward. I can't be bothered with that.

MR WALSH

If you could have another three wishes, would you have them?

JACKY

Not me. I learned my lesson. You know the old saying..."be

Careful what you wish for...you may just get it?" In fact, I should just chuck it in the fire...there! I've been meaning to do that.

MR WALSH

Billy! Why did you do that?

JACKY

Better to let it burn.

MR WALSH

If you don't want it, give it to me. I'll get it...

JACKY

No, don't! I threw it on the fire.

MR WALSH

Got it! It's still good.

JACKY

If you keep it, don't blame me for what happens. Throw it back on the fire like a sensible man.

MR WALSH

Oh come on now. I'm being sensible. How do you do it?

JACKY

Alright. If you insist. Hold it up in your right hand, and wish aloud. But, I warn you of the consequences.

MRS WALSH

Sounds like something out of the Arabian Nights. I'm off to clean the dishes. Why don't you wish for four pairs of hands for me?

MR WALSH

Alright..

JACKY

No!

MR WALSH

I was only fooling.

JACKY

Don't even fool with it. If you must...wish for something sensible.

MR WALSH

Sensible! What does that mean? Where are you going?

JACKY

I have to be off now.

MRS WALSH

Already? You just got here.

JACKY

Must catch an early morning train. Just wanted to stop by before I ship out to Zanzibar.

MR WALSH

Zanzibar! Did you hear that? He's going to Zanzibar!

MRS WALSH

I heard, I heard. Now, if you hear from our Bobby, you tell him to keep writing. I'm going to complain to our post office about the slow service.

JACKY

I'll tell him.   Please, be careful with that thing...goodbye!

MR WALSH

Goodbye! Stay safe!

(DOOR CLOSE)

MRS WALSH

Did you give him anything for the trinket?

MR WALSH

It's not a trinket. It's a talisman. That's what it is. He didn't want it. He let me have it. Sort of a souvenir from another part of the world. I guess we'll never see any place but this godforsaken....

MRS WALSH
Well, rub your trinket and make a wish...make us rich and famous. Then we can go anywhere we like. We can go to Paris and see Bobby.

MR WALSH
He said to be sensible with our wishes.

MRS WALSH
I was only fooling with you, George. Come on, let's get ready for bed.

MR WALSH
Alright, I'll be in, in a second. Hmmm...I wouldn't want to be greedy. All we need is about a thousand dollars for a new truck and a tractor and... I mean, that's not much to ask. No harm in that. Alright, then...just for fun, I'm going to wish...I wish for a thousand dollars. (Screams) Aaaahhhh!

MRS WALSH
Good lord! What happened?

MR WALSH
It moved! It squirmed in my hand, twisted like a snake! I'm telling you, it moved about on its own! I wished for a thousand dollars and...it wiggled and...

MRS WALSH
Well, I don't see any money lying about. You must have imagined it. Too much whiskey I'm sure.

MR WALSH
Never mind. No harm done. But it gave me a shock all the same.

MRS WALSH
I suppose you'll find the cash tied up in a big bag in the middle of your bed. And something horrible hiding in your closet watching you as you pocket your ill-gotten gains. Ha!

MR WALSH

I know what I felt. I haven't been drinking. Much. That damned thing moved. Squirming like it was alive. A monkey's paw, that's what it is. Like a little hand, grabbing me. I can feel its tiny finger nails digging into my hand.

MRS WALSH

(Off) Come to bed!

(MUSIC)

MR WALSH

Ah, well, the sun has finally come out!

MRS WALSH

It's a beautiful day.

MR WALSH

Where is it? The hand? Ah, there it is...right where I dropped it last night. Dirty, little, shriveled thing, isn't it? In the light of day...it's not so enchanting.

MRS WALSH

Believing in such nonsense! Wishing for a thousand dollars! You ought to have your head examined.

MR WALSH

Well, it gave us a moment of entertainment, at least. A little fantasy in our humdrum life. But, I swear the thing did move in my hand. I didn't imagine it. Oh well. I'll put it on the mantel here. Sort of a curio. Maybe, I'll make a little wooden stand for it. Or a plaque.

MRS WALSH

George! There's someone coming up the path from the road.

MR WALSH

A man?

MRS WALSH

It's a soldier...in uniform...oh, dear Lord!

(KNOCK, DOOR OPEN)

Hello.

CORPORAL

Mrs. Walsh?

MRS WALSH

Yes. Can I help you?

CORPORAL

I'm Corporal Benjamin Farley, Sixteenth Regiment, U.S.Army…

MRS WALSH

It's about our Bobby! Oh no…no…

MR WALSH

Oh, hush! The war's been over for a month. What is it son?

CORPORAL

Well, I'm afraid to tell you…your son, Private Robert Benjamin
Walsh…had been reported missing in action during the last
battle…

MR WALSH

We had no word of this. Why weren't we notified?

MRS WALSH

Oh! Jesus, Mary and Joseph!

CORPORAL

I apologize for the United States Army, sir. But, the whole
continent over there is in a state of disarray. The thing is…I'm
sorry to tell you, his remains was discovered three days ago
and his body will be shipped back here within a week.

MRS WALSH

Dead! Bobby is dead!

CORPORAL

In the meantime, I have been ordered to give you this package
of his belongings…and a check for a thousand dollars which
was left in his Army savings account.

MR WALSH

A thousand...dollars?

MRS WALSH

My little boy! Dead! Oh dear Lord, no!

CORPORAL

I'm sorry to be the one to bring you the bad news. I have to be moving along now...I have many more names on my list. Again, the U.S.Army expresses its deepest sorrow over your loss.

MR WALSH

Yes...yes...thank you. Good by.

(DOOR CLOSE)

A thousand dollars.

MRS WALSH

My poor little soldier. Why? After the war is over...why?

MR WALSH

It's out of our hands, dear. He's with the Lord now. There's nothing we could have done. It's fate. Nothing but...but...a thousand dollars.

MRS WALSH

That's all you can think about at a time like this? Money?

MR WALSH

No! Don't you see? The monkey's paw! I wished for a thousand dollars!

MRS WALSH

Stop staring at that damned paw. What's got into you? It's only a coincidence. It has to be.

MR WALSH

Billy warned us. He said it would bring us grief. Reward with grief.

MRS WALSH

Well, staring at that thing isn't going to do any good.

MR WALSH

It isn't? No...I suppose not. Well, we're all alone now, Martha. Our only boy...gone to Heaven before us. It's not right. It's not right.

MRS WALSH

I told him not to go. I pleaded for him not to sign up.

MR WALSH

Don't you see? It was meant to be.

MRS WALSH

Oh! We'll never see him again...never again...I wasn't even there to hold his hand when he died.

MR WALSH

It must have been quick, dear. I'm sure. It must've been. He didn't suffer. He was fighting for his country, remember that. A hero, he is. Our boy...

MRS WALSH

To die so far off, away from us.

MR WALSH

They'll be bringing him back to us next week, he said. You wait and see. The whole town will honor him.

MRS WALSH

Who cares? The whole town can go to hell. The whole country. I...I feel so empty inside...I miss him. I want to be with him. I don't want to live anymore.

MR WALSH

Don't talk like that. Life goes on. We must be proud of our boy. Let's be off to bed...we've got the rest of our lives to mourn him.

MRS WALSH

Do you think I can go to sleep now?

MR WALSH

We'll need our rest. There will be much to do when our son comes home to us. We have to make sure he gets the proper recognition. A decent funeral. We'll use the money here to...

MRS WALSH

Wait! The paw! The monkey's paw!

MR WALSH

What's the matter?

MRS WALSH

I want it. You haven't destroyed it?

MR WALSH

It's in the parlor, on the mantel. Why?

MRS WALSH

Don't you see? Why didn't I think of it before? Why didn't you think of it?

MR WALSH

Think of what?

MRS WALSH

The other two wishes. We've only had one.

MR WALSH

Wasn't that enough?

MRS WALSH

No. We'll have one more.

MR WALSH

You're not thinking...?

MRS WALSH

We'll wish our boy alive again.

MR WALSH

Now Martha...even if that were so....

MRS WALSH

Get it, get it quickly, and wish ...Oh my boy, my boy!

MR.WALSH

Get to bed. You don't know what you're saying.

MRS WALSH

You had the first wish granted...why not the second?

MR WALSH

A coincidence. You said so yourself.

MRS WALSH

Go get it and wish!

MR WALSH

He has been dead over a week, and besides he...well, who knows what had happened to him? A bomb? Machine gun, whatever? He might be a sorry sight. Listen to me, talking like this...I'm the one going mad.

MRS WALSH

Bring him back! Do you think I fear my own child? If there's one thing you ever do worthwhile in your sorry life, George Walsh, wish our boy back to life!

MR WALSH

Alright! But, it's against the laws of God and nature. Here it is. This stupid paw. Look at me, trembling like a leaf. This is ridiculous.

JACKY (VO ECHO)

Be careful what you wish for, you may get it...

MRS WALSH

Wish!

MR WALSH

This is madness!

MRS WALSH

Wish!

MR WALSH

I wish my son... alive again. (Screams) Aaahhh! It moved again! It's on the floor. I can't take any more of this. Where are you going?

MRS WALSH

To the window. I'm going to light a candle. And wait.
(MUSIC, CLOCK TICKS, STRIKES)

MR WALSH

It's been three hours, Martha. Come to bed. It's nearly morning. You'll catch a cold sitting there in the dark by the window.

(SOFT KNOCK)

MRS WALSH

What was that? Did you hear it?

MR WALSH

Yes. I did. Must be a shutter knocking in the wind.

MRS WALSH

Was it the door?

MR WALSH

No.

(LOUD KNOCK)

MRS WALSH

The door! Someone at the door. It's him! I know it! It's my boy!

MR WALSH

Come back! What are you going to do? For God's sake, don't let him in!

MRS WALSH

What are you doing? Let go of me! Let go! I must open the door! Are you afraid of your own son?

(KNOCKING)

I'm coming, son! Mommy is coming! Let go, George!
(FURNITURE CRASH)

MR.WALSH

Please come back! Stop!

(BOLT OPENS ON DOOR)

The paw! The paw! Where is it? Here it is...

(KNOCKING)

MRS WALSH

I'm coming, Bobby!

MR WALSH

I wish...my dead son to return to the beyond!

(DOOR OPENS, WIND HOWLS)

MRS WALSH

Bobby! Bobby! Where are you, son? Bobby? There's no one here...but, look...

(THUNDER)

MR WALSH

Must have been the wind...a loose window shutter...

MRS WALSH

No! Oh God no! Look...look at the ground, the mud... footprints...coming down the path and...

MR WALSH

Footprints...leading right up to our door.

MRS WALSH

He was here, George! He was here! But, why...where did he go? What...? What's that you have in your hand, George? The paw! There was a third wish left and... you didn't!

MR WALSH

I had to. I had to! I had to!

MRS WALSH

You...wished our son...*away?* Back, into the cold, dark, abyss...? How dare you...!

MR WALSH

I *had* to. Don't you see?

MRS WALSH

You did it...

MR WALSH

Now, Martha...think of it...it's not right. Not natural. He was dead, Martha...in his coffin. God knows what condition he was in. Martha? Why are you look at me like that? Martha...put that knife down! Put it down, I say! Martha, no! (Screams) Aaaahhhh!

RAIN
By Dan Bianchi
From A Story By Dana Burnet

Cast – 3m, 1w
Running Time – 15 min
Synopsis – A woman can no longer stand her boring life and husband

(THUNDER, RAIN)

NARRATOR

For days, the rain's been falling steadily, monotonously, relentlessly. It's like the sky is a grey mask covering the face of God. In all the world there is no sound but the drip, drip, drip of rain. Allie Baird stands at her bedroom window, dressed only in a white slip, her long yellow hair falling over her shoulders. She stares out at the little Maine fishing village, huddled against the sky, and beyond it the drab reach of the sea. A cluster of wet roofs and the lone steeple standing amongst them, like a tombstone dominating a graveyard.

ALLIE

I hate that steeple.

NARRATOR

It belongs to the church in which she was married. She stands shivering with the cold, remembering. The naked wooden altar…the voice of the melancholy minister pronouncing sentence upon her soul …feeling the cold hand of Jim Baird fumbling for her hand…the even colder embrace of the ring upon her finger.

ALLIE

It had rained *that* day, too, as it is raining now. Eighteen years ago!

NARRATOR

And, in all that time, only three things of importance have happened to her… first, the birth of her child… second, the death of her child… and, third, a trip to Portland for a minor operation. Except for these events…

ALLIE

My life...

NARRATOR

Her life has been a barren desert of days.

(MAN GROANS)

In the bed behind her, a man stirring, grunting. She gazes down at her husband. His huge body beneath the tumbled coverings... his face with its stubble of beard appears hideous against the untidy pillow. His small eyes leer up at her with that maddening lifelessness, that indifferent stare which has begun to sicken her.

JIM

Still raining, Allie?

ALLIE

Still raining.

NARRATOR

He's asked that question every morning for a week, and she answers in the same way. But this morning her voice trembles.

JIM

You'll catch your death goin' about in your underwear. Why don't you get your clothes on like a sensible woman?

ALLIE

Yeah.

JIM

Ain't no use getting up awhile. Can't go anywhere in rain like this. Like being in jail. Wake me when breakfast's ready.

ALLIE

Yeah.

NARRATOR

She dresses listlessly, in silence.

(SNORING)

She goes swiftly out of the room, her hair still hanging loosely down her back. Entering the kitchen, she sets about the business of getting breakfast, only pausing to sip a cup of coffee. Again, she stares out the window, her eyes fixed upon the distant grey blur of ocean that forms the horizon of her world. Suddenly…

ALLIE

What's that?

NARRATOR

Out there…a sail upon the far water…like a drenched moth struggling through the rain.

JIM

Hey Allie, you've burnt the bacon! Thought I smelled it burning. Just like you, always lookin' out the window and not mindin' your housework…

ALLIE

I thought I saw a sail, Jim.

JIM

Ha! A sail? So, what if you did? Ain't nothin' to get excited about, is it?

ALLIE

Look, Jim, isn't that a schooner out there…off the Point?

JIM

Where? I don't see no sail.

ALLIE

You never see the things I see, do you, Jim?

JIM

All I said is, I don't see no schooner off the Point, not in this weather. And, you don't neither, though you're always sayin' you do. Soon as you get a little fidgety, you begin seeing ships off the Point. What are you looking for? Huh? (Pause) Anyway, you always was careless and wasteful, Allie, look at

at all this burnt bacon. Careless and wasteful…with bacon
bacon costin' what it does.

ALLIE
It doesn't cost as much as whiskey!

JIM
Now, Allie…

ALLIE
Whiskey's ruined you, Jim Baird… not my carelessness.

JIM
Hey now, who's saying, I'm ruined? Not me. My delivery job
still pays expenses, and a little left over. And as for what you
said…you know I ain't no heavy drinker.

ALLIE
I wish to God you were! I wish you'd go out and get drunk like
a man and come home and beat me if you wanted to! It's this
everlasting taking it, taking it, taking
it, drinking behind my back…and then lyin' to yourself to ease
your conscience.

JIM
Now, Allie, you know that ain't true. You know I'm subject to
colds. The doctor said a drop or two wouldn't hurt me…

ALLIE
He didn't say to drink a bottle a week!

JIM
I ain't drunk a bottle. There's some men… Now, Allie, you know
I need a tonic. This house's chilled through. The weather's
been terrible, plain murderous.

ALLIE
Don't say that word!

NARRATOR
She stands over him, her bosom heaving, a pitiful frightened
helplessness in her eyes. It's as though she recognizes her

growing inability to struggle against fate. Jim Baird looks at her with the faint bravado that is his cloak of cowardice... then he just sits down at the table and begins to eat, while Allie watches him with a strange horror. Her loathing of him has grown considerably in recent months. Look at him, eating like a beast. This week of bad weather is bringing to the surface many of her hidden emotions, her secret opinions, her long-concealed hatreds. The endless drip of the rain has begun to wear upon her calloused spirit... to grate her nerves. She can't remember when she's been shut up with him, under one roof, for such a long time.

ALLIE
I wish you hadn't said it was murderous weather.

JIM
What?

NARRATOR
After breakfast, he goes into the front room...a pathetic dreary chamber filled with cheap nick-nacks pretending to give the place a cheerful ambiance. They fail miserably. From a small cabinet he takes a bottle and drinks...not recklessly, but, rather stingily. Can't imbibe more than is necessary to intoxicate him. He's on a budget. He fills his pipe and sits down by the window. Allie moves slowly about the kitchen, prolonging, as far as possible, the washing of the dishes. At last, she picks up the carving knife, a long sharp-bladed affair, and begins to scour it with trembling hands. There is an appalling commotion in her heart. The frightened look has returned to her eyes. Suddenly, the knife falls clattering to the floor. With an air of grim determination she walks into the front room and sits down at her husband's side.

ALLIE
Jim...I...I want to talk to you.

JIM
All right, Allie, talk ahead. I guess you're lonesome...is that it?

ALLIE

That's it, Jim. I'm lonesome. And it doesn't seem right, somehow. It doesn't seem natural. We're husband and wife, Jim, and...we ought...to... talk...more. We ought to talk about...

JIM

The weather?

ALLIE

God...no!

JIM

Then, what, Allie?

ALLIE

Well, what do other husbands and wives talk about, when they're shut in together? Are they all like this? If they are, then they're nothing but *prisoners*!

JIM

Now, Allie...

ALLIE

You've got to talk to me, Jim. You've got to find something we can share, something we can take an interest in. All our lives we've gone along like this. We're strangers, after eighteen years, and it's...killing me! Oh, Jim, if you'd only try to be a man! If you'd only quit drinking and go to work again. I mean *real work*, work that *means* something. I'll help you, Jim! I'll work with you...

JIM

Why, Allie, what's come over you? Ain't you got three meals a day, and a good bed to sleep in?

ALLIE

Yes, but that's not living. That's just keeping your body warm. I want something else, something I can look forward to...a trip to Portland maybe, or a new dress, or maybe...

JIM

Ha! Ha! Ha! Allie Baird wants a new dress! A trip to Portland!

That's what it's all about, eh? I knew there was somethin' on your mind besides the weather. Buying things for yourself! (Angry) God A'mighty, ain't I got troubles enough without havin' a greedy wife?

NARRATOR
He rises from his chair, facing her in a sullen fury. She draws back slowly, her arm half lifted as though to ward off a blow. But, still, she clings to the hopeless dream of making him see, of making him understand.

ALLIE
It isn't that, Jim! I swear it isn't that! I don't care about having those things. I only want something that we can take pleasure in...and...and...

JIM
You lie, Allie Baird! Get back into that kitchen and be thankful you ain't walkin' the streets in the rain.

NARRATOR
Her arms fall to her sides... a dry sob escapes her lips. She turns and walks wearily from the room. In the kitchen, she sinks down by the window, and puts her head on her arms. It seems as though the rain has stopped at last.

(MUSIC)

Look! In the orchard behind the rambling old farmhouse, a young girl walks with her lover. The air is sweet with the fragrance of apple-blossoms. The twilight has come. It's a kingdom of shadows, now. Infinite solitudes, where they might wander in peace and safety. The man is fair- haired, blue-eyed...he walks proudly like a young Viking. He's sailing at daybreak for England. It's to be his last trip before they're married. He tightens his arm around her waist.

MAN
You'll be standin' at the window and you'll see my ship roundin' the Point...you can tell her by the canvas she carries! And you'll put on the ring I gave you, for you'll know it's Hartley Taylor comin' home for his sweetheart.

NARRATOR

Swaying against him, she whispers…

ALLIE

But, what if you shouldn't come?

NARRATOR

He takes her in his arms and kisses her.

MAN

I'll come one way or another. One way or another. Wait for me always.

NARRATOR

He leaves at dawn, in the schooner. She stands at the window, his ring against her lips, watching his sails until they show no more. …

(MUSIC)

A week later the remnants of the fishing fleet come driving home in the teeth of the gale… but, Hartley Taylor does not come, though she watches the Point night and day, all the long winter through. And, when the spring comes again, and her heart is dead in her breast, she goes down to the edge of the great water, and gives his ring to the sea. …The following June, at the urgent request of both her father and mother, she marries Jim Baird, who wants a wife, and is willing to trade for one upon a purely business basis.

(THUNDER, RAIN)

ALLIE

Oh dear…what am I doing? Thinking, seeing things. The past. Staring out to the sea. Maybe I didn't see a sail after all. Maybe, I'm just seeing things.

NARRATOR

The ceaseless patter of rain at the window stirs her to full consciousness. Her relaxed nerves tighten. Her brain throbs. She keeps fighting off that thought that's gnawing at her… ever since dawn. So, she cooks dinner, and sits in her chair, by the window while Jim Baird eats. She, herself, does not taste food. The carving knife still lays on the floor between them until Jim picks it up.

> JIM

What the hell? Careless…careless…here, what's this doing on the floor?

> NARRATOR

He returns to the front room. Now, he drinks more boldly With a false courage born of hate. Allie's plea has shaken him from that numbing lethargy…that refuge, that shelter into which he has crept…to protect him from her passionate demands and life itself! How dare she accuse him… how dare she…? He rages within. It's not long before he's thoroughly drunk.

> ALLIE

Jim! Come to supper.

> NARRATOR

He comes alright, reeling, falling into his chair with a loud laugh that echoes mockingly throughout the silent house.

> JIM

Ha!

> NARRATOR

For some moments, he smiles to himself, makes jests about the rain…

> JIM

Forty days of rain, you know? The Bible! Forty days…it's the end of the world!

> NARRATOR

Allie sits with her back toward him, her body rigid, her hands gripping the chair. Finally he rises and approaches her.

> JIM

What? You told me t' get drunk…and beat you… remember?

(SLAP)

How's that? Bitch. Come t' the table. Ain't right t' turn your
back on your husband. Ain't natural.

NARRATOR

To his own maudlin amazement, she does exactly as he
commands. She sits down opposite him, leans her elbows on
the table, and looks at him with a smile. It's a smile that lights
her whole countenance, strange radiance
caused by something burning within her breast. It's as
though in striking her he has kindled a slumbering spark to
flame. Her eyes gleam. Her cheeks are flushed as with a fever.
For the first time in eighteen years, Allie does not wash the
supper dishes.

JIM

I'm going out!

(DOOR CLOSE)

NARRATOR

As soon as he's gone, she goes upstairs and puts on her white
dress...the only one she owns besides her monotonous
gingham. ...Then she returns to the kitchen, turns out the light,
and waits for Jim Baird to come home.
The lighthouse on the Point has begun to glow. She keeps her
gaze upon that distant flame. It steadies her. The rain falls
monotonously, as it has fallen for days...as it has fallen for
ages!

(MUSIC, DOOR CLOSE,
FOOTSTEPS STAIRS)

Hours later, he returns. Growling in the dark. Still she waits, in
her white dress, her hair down her back. Time, that had seemed
so interminable to her this morning, is now an inconsequential
trifle.

(CLOCK STRIKES THREE)

It's time. She rises from her chair, picks up the long-bladed
knife and slowly mounts the stairs. As she enters the
bedroom, a reek of whiskey attacks her nostrils. She feels,
rather than sees, her husband's huge bulk upon the bed.
Sleeping, sleeping the deep sleep of drunkenness

and he whimpers a little as he breathes. She creeps closer, leaning down and kissing him. She whispers…

ALLIE

Poor Jim!

NARRATOR

Then lifting the knife high in the air, she drives it home.
(MUSIC STING)

She reaches the open window…somehow…and kneeling before it, her arms across the sill …she sees…she sees…

ALLIE

A ship…it's coming for me… through the rain. A schooner…

NARRATOR

A schooner with all its sails plunging through the grey sea of the mist… a white shape afloat upon the air. The woman at the window smiles, and reaches into her bosom for the ring her lover had given her… but, the ring is not there. Then, she glances once more at the oncoming ship, and sees Hartley Taylor standing at the lee-rail, with the ring in his hand, and the light of its single stone filling the world with glory!

MAN

I'll come…one way or another!

NARRATOR

She feels the light upon her face, upon her hair…and holds out her hands to him in greeting, crying his name across the shriveled waters.
(SILENCE, GROAN, YAWN)

JIM

Has it stopped rainin', Allie?

NARRATOR

There is no reply. He glances toward the window, and sees her kneeling at the sill. In a brilliant flood of sunshine…her head upon her arms and her yellow hair falling about her shoulders like so much spun gold.

JIM

Now, Allie, you'll catch your death…

NARRATOR

Something in her stillness checks the words on his lips.

JIM

Allie?

NARRATOR

He gets awkwardly out of bed, his face a mottled grey, and walks slowly toward the kneeling figure. Suddenly he halts, and stares panic-stricken at a dark stain on the floor …

JIM

Jesus Christ…

NARRATOR

His legs give way beneath him. He sinks into a chair, a growing horror in his eyes.

JIM

Just like you, Allie…Couldn't stand a little bad weather. …If you'd just waited another day. … Sun's out now!

NARRATOR

He looks once more at that still figure by the window… sees the light on her hair, feels the immeasurable distance between them. Then, he begins to sob weakly.

(SOBBING)

THE SCREAMING SKULL
By Dan Bianchi
From A Story By F.Marion Crawford.

Cast – 3m, 1w
Running Time – 20 min
Synopsis – A dead woman's skull haunts a man

(BLOOD CURDLING SCREAM)

NARRATOR

"Oh yes, I have often heard it scream. No, I'm not the nervous sort. Nor, am I imagining things. And, I've never believed in ghosts...unless that thing is one. Whatever it is, it hates me almost as much as it hated Luke Pratt. Believe it or not, the damned thing...it screams at me. My fault. I should have known. Never discuss ingenious ways of killing people in public. You never can tell if someone listening might get the idea that they want to do away with their nearest and dearest. I blame myself for Gloria's death. I suppose I was responsible for it in a way. If I had not told that particular true story she might yet be alive. No wonder the damned thing still screams at me.

"The truth is, I had no idea that the doctor and his wife were not on good terms. They used to bicker a bit, now and then. Gloria would hold her temper and bite her lip, while Luke would say the most offensive things. He was always like that. He was my cousin. That is how I inherited this house. After he died, he left it to me. Yes, it's a nice little place. Nice garden. Especially when the rhododendrons are in bloom.

"Anyway, let me tell you how all of this came about. It was a wet night last November. The rain was coming down in buckets. A Nor'easter was howling outside. So, here I am having dinner with Luke and Gloria when suddenly Luke, who is in a bad mood, stands up and throws his food aside.

PRATT

Don't you know? My wife is trying to poison me! She'll succeed some day.

NARRATOR

"Alright, Gloria isn't much of a cook.   But, I can see that she's
hurt, and I try to make light of it all."   Oh, Luke, she's much
too clever to get rid of you in such a simple way. Now, not too
long ago, there was a woman in Ireland who had killed off three
husbands before anyone suspected her. Her fourth husband
managed to catch her and she was hanged. Turns out, she
had drugged the other husbands and poured melted lead into
their ears through a little funnel.

PRATT

Didn't they have autopsies?

NARRATOR

I guess so, I don't know.   "Well, I didn't think much about it,
but…here's the thing…three days later, Gloria dies suddenly in
her bed. Natural causes. Ahem. My cousin Luke becomes a
widower. He doesn't mourn her death much…but, I can see
that he is very upset about something. Now, Gloria had this
old dog named Bumble, a bull dog. Very sweet. Followed her
everywhere. A week after she passed away, I ask Luke…"
Luke, I haven't seen Bumble about.   Has he run away?

PRATT

No. I…killed him. I couldn't stand it any longer. He had a way
of sitting in *her* chair and glaring at me. And the howling. He
wouldn't stop.   He didn't suffer at all, poor old Bumble. I put
dionine into his drink to make him sleep. It's been quieter ever
since.

NARRATOR

That's odd. Bumble had never howled before.

PRATT

No…he hadn't.   By the way…that story you told that night at
dinner, the one about the Irish woman who killed her
husbands…what ever happened to her?

NARRATOR

What? Oh, that. Well, I believe that the authorities eventually
dug up the three skulls of the previous

husbands and they found a small lump of lead rattling about in each skull. She had poured that hot lead into their ears and melted a hole through their brains. Instantaneous death. That was all the evidence they needed to hang the woman.

PRATT

I see.

NARRATOR

"Now I'm wondering…did Luke kill his wife? Where's the proof? Unless… well…there is the ladle. A big soup ladle. I found it in the closet in the bedroom. It has some kind of hard, gray stuff stuck to it. Lead, I think. But, that proves nothing. Luke may have had a dozen reasons for melting a little lead in a ladle. Now, don't get me wrong. Luke Pratt is dead and gone. I don't want to stir up anything that will hurt his memory. They are both dead. Both…died horribly. Yes, when Luke was found dead on the beach, the Sheriff discovered hideous marks on his throat…"

SHERIFF

He wasn't robbed. But, I'd say he was murdered…by the hands or teeth of some person or animal unknown. Odd, though. Just lying there…on his back with that old cardboard box next to him. Empty, it was. And sitting there on his back…was that skull.

NARRATOR

What skull?

SHERIFF

Well, he was a doctor, right? They probably carry such things about with them. It must have rolled out of the box when he was attacked. It was a remarkably fine skull. Not very old. Very white with perfect teeth. But, no lower jaw.

NARRATOR

Where is it now?

SHERIFF

Well, we didn't need it for evidence. I put it up on a shelf in the doctor's hall closet back in his house. Odd thing was…

NARRATOR

What?

SHERIFF

Well…somebody must have taken that skull and put it on the dead man's back, I guess. It's not like it could jump out of the box and get in that position all by itself. Why would someone do that? Odd, very odd. But, that's a fact.

NARRATOR

"Now, I'm no believer in the supernatural. There may be ghosts, I don't know. I feel it's a waste of time and energy in all the universe for a dead spirit to go about scaring people. But, now…I begin to feel a sort of eerie feeling about the whole thing. I mean…it may be a stretch of my imagination…but, can it be that the mysterious skull belongs to Gloria Pratt, herself? Alright, alright, I know that she's buried in the churchyard. But, why…? I mean, it's monstrous to suppose her husband kept her skull in an old cardboard box in his hall closet. Was Luke insane? If it was, *is*, her skull, then, obviously, he must have killed her just like the way the Irish woman did to her three husbands. Remember, when I told him how the authorities disinterred the bodies and discovered the evil deed? Yes, he didn't want that to happen to him some day, so…as a doctor, he might have just removed her head before she was buried.

"Well, as his only living relative, I inherited the Pratt house and everything in it. Odd? You want to hear something odd? I now own that skull. I've tried to get rid of the damned thing, but, it doesn't like that. It wants to be there in its place, in that cardboard box in the hall closet. It's not happy anywhere else. And, as I've said…it *screams*. Yes, it goes on all night. It does no good to
remove it from the house. And, I'm not the only one who hears it. I can't get anyone from the village to work for me. As for selling the place, or even renting it, that's out of the question.

"Now, I may be all wrong about the skull. Maybe it's a lab specimen and it's only a piece of clay or something rattling inside it. If it is a lump of lead…then, I feel I may be to blame. As long as I don't know for certain…

(MOAN)

"There! There it is again! I must have been thinking bad thoughts about it. It knows, believe me. Doesn't like that stuff. That's just a moan. That's nothing. It gets much worse than that, believe me. When I had first heard it, it was a low moan...in the closet in the box. For nights on end. Keeping me awake. I'm not so much afraid, but annoyed. But, lately, the voice...I suppose you can call it that...it's growing louder. Last night, I ran in, grabbed the box and chucked it out the window.

(GLASS CRASH)

"Then my hair stood on end. The thing screamed unbearably as it flew through the air into the darkness below. I didn't get much sleep after that. I got up, smoking my pipe, pacing the floor. With that thing screaming outside, getting closer.

(KNOCK)

"Someone at the door?" Hold on, I'm coming!

(OPENS DOOR, WIND)

"No one there. So, I stand there in the open doorway, peering out into the night. And then...something rolls against my foot. I don't move a muscle. I know what it is before I look down. I pick the thing up carefully. I'm in a daze. I don't want anyone to see me with it. I light a candle and place it on the table. The flickering light and shadow play tricks on me. The empty eye sockets appear to be opening and closing. I'm quaking with fear. Shivering. Especially when the candle light goes out. The thing has come home. I carry it back to the hall closet. I even speak to it..." You'll have your cardboard box back in the morning.

"Am I crazy, or, did that damned thing crawl around to the front of the house and knock to be let in? How? It's just a skull, for God's sakes! Look, I'll just put it back in the closet. In its cardboard box. After that, things will calm down awhile.

(MUSIC)

"Weeks pass. I'm able to hire a maid, Mrs.McMurtry. New to this town, the rumors about this place don't frighten her."

MCMURTRY

I know all about this house's reputation, sir, but, I've spent
quite a few years in a real haunted mansion with a dozen
ghosts...there's nothing that can scare me away.

NARRATOR

"She stays for several months of peace and quiet. One day
while she is out working in the garden, she's digging around
and finds...the missing jaw bone to the skull. Buried in a pit of
quicklime."

MCMURTRY

Maybe it fits that skull that's in the cupboard upstairs,
sir? Maybe Dr Pratt had put the skull into the lime to clean it,
or something, and when he took it out he left the lower jaw
behind. There's some human hair sticking in the lime, sir.

NARRATOR

"Now, I wonder, why is Mrs.McMurtry suggesting such a thing,
if she does not suspect something? Perhaps, she knows more
than she cares to tell?"

MCMURTRY

Do you want me to bring it over to the churchyard and give it a
proper burial?

NARRATOR

No, I'll take it.   "Imagine how cold a person has to be...not
just to kill another living soul, but, then, to live with the
remains? I take the jaw back into the house and fit it to the
skull and...OW! It bit me! It bit me...Maybe, it's my
nerves...that's it, I'm a bit high strung....but now, I recall what
the Sheriff had said about Luke's death...

SHERIFF

...by the hand or teeth of some person or animal
unknown.

NARRATOR

"I can feel it now. It's alive and trying to bite me. The skull, I
know it hates me. It still has something rattling

around inside it. I hold the box. I don't want to shake it, the jaw might get separated from it again, and I'm sure it won't like that.

(SCREAM)

"There, did you hear that? That's not coming from the box certainly. Definitely comes from somewhere else. Is it the wind whistling down the chimney like in those ghost stories? Not the skull at all. Well, I'll open the box, and we'll take it out and look at it under the bright light, shall we? Just think, the poor woman whose skull this was...she used to sit right there in that chair.

(SCREAM, WIND, CRASH)

"Ahh...you hear that? Was that...? No, it's the wind.... must be the wind. Terrible gust of wind...the door flew open...the wind knocked the vase over...Sure, it's always been the wind. Letting my imagination run away with me. It can't be the skull. The skull is locked in the box sitting on the table. But, that scream, I mean, the wind...it came from outside. Obviously, the skull can't be in two places at once, right? The box has been sealed with tape and string. I'll just cut the seal here and open the lid and remove the...*what!* There's nothing in here! It's empty! The skull...it's gone! Somebody must have tampered with the seal. They stole the skull. Mrs.McMurtry! Of course. If not her, then...no, I won't even think otherwise. That's crazy. On the other hand...I did find it on the front step that night. I mean, suppose it's on the loose now and...in the house here now, waiting for me in some dark corner? Hunting me? Suppose it screams bloody murder again? Wait...what's this? There's something in the bottom of the box. A ball of lead. I was right. Luke did kill his wife with it. I'm sure of it. A lump of lead. Think of what it did. Makes me tremble. He gave her something to make her sleep, of course. The dionine he gave the dog to put it to sleep for good! Oh, Gloria! I'm so sorry. I didn't mean for this to happen. That moment of awful agony. Having boiling lead poured into your brain. Think of it. She was dead before she could scream...

(SCREAM)

"It's just outside this room...I can't keep it out of my head! Just a noise. A noise never hurt anybody, right? Well, if I'm to get any peace, I need to find that skull and get it back in the box on the shelf where it belongs. Bury it? Yes, if I can find it, I'll bury it. Reunite it with it's body, that's it! Six feet deep and cover it up. It'll never get out again. I must be losing my mind. Have to get hold of myself. I know... I'll get the lantern and I'll go looking for it.

(KNOCKS)

"I've heard that knock before. It wants to come in and be taken upstairs in its box. I know, I'll capture it. I'll hold the box...and put it in. No, I need to hold the box open...and I'll open the door, too. I just....Stop that knocking! I hear you out there! Ready...one, two, three...

(DOOR CREAKS)

"Get it! Get it! It's over there...over there! Watch out!

(DOOR SLAM)

"Easy now, don't be rough with it. It doesn't like that, you know. *Ow!* Damn! It bit me! Alright, alright, we'll fix that...put some ointment on it. Look there. There's a drop of blood on the upper jaw. It's on the eyetooth. That's frightening. Ha! Did you see when it was moving along the floor...I thought I was going to drop dead from fright. Go ahead wipe off that blood. I'm going to really seal up the box this time. And, I'll put a lock on that closet, too. You won't be going anywhere, my dear. You fat, hum drum, boring, ignorant bitch! If you think you run things around here, you've got another thing coming! First thing tomorrow...yes, first thing tomorrow, I'll... (Screams) Aaaaahhhhh!

(SKULL SCREAMS, MUSIC, SIREN)

SHERIFF

You say the body wasn't moved.

MCMURTRY

No, Sir...it's exactly the way I found it. Just laying there in bed.

SHERIFF
Strange. Looks like he's been bitten in the throat...those are marks made by human teeth...but, whoever did it must have used amazing force...The windpipe is completely crushed. I'd say that was the cause of death. Yes, death by the hands or teeth of some person unknown. I'd even go so far as to say...yes, by the looks of those marks, the small size of the jaws...I'd say that the maniac is a woman. He didn't have a wife, did he? An ex-wife, perhaps?

MCMURTRY
No, sir, he was all alone.

SHERIFF
That's strange. That looks like the same skull we found next to Luke Pratt's body... And he was killed in the same way. I remember putting that skull away in a box up on the closet shelf. I wonder what it's doing here? Hmmmm....it's a mystery...

MCMURTRY
That's what it is, sir. A bonafide mystery.

SHERIFF
Well, I guess I'll take this skull down to the jailhouse as evidence and lock it in the safe...

(DISTANT SCREAM)

Listen! Did you hear that?

MCMURTRY
What?

SHERIFF
Oh...nothing, nothing. Must be the wind...

THE JUDGE'S HOUSE
By Dan Bianchi
From A Story By Bram Stoker

Cast – 1m, 1w
Running Time – 15 min
Synopsis – A student rents a house haunted by a terrible judge

(MUSIC)

NARRATOR
"I had to get away. I need time to study without all the distractions. Without my friends. I have to go somewhere alone in secret so no one knows where I am. So, I packed my books and baggage and bought a train ticket to a place I've never seen before. A little village called Stony Brook where I've rented an old house out on Post Road. The owner was only too glad to give me a great price...he said that the house has stood empty for years. He didn't tell me why. So, when I spoke to the woman who runs the general store in the village...

WOMAN
You're living in the Judge's House?

NARRATOR
The Judge's House?

WOMAN
That's what the town folk call it. The Judge's House.

NARRATOR
What about the place?

WOMAN
It's called that because many years ago...I think it was a hundred years ago...it was the home of a judge...a terrifying judge who gave harsh sentences to prisoners. He'd stand there in his red robe with a fur collar and point to the defendant and point his finger and pronounce his sentence of death. All the while, smiling like a fiend. They say, he didn't care much if the victim was innocent or not. Sent a lot of people to the gallows.

NARRATOR
So, what's that got to do with the house?

WOMAN
All I know is…I wouldn't stay one night in there if you paid me all the money in the world. Anyway, nevermind, what I say. I'm sorry I even brought it up to a young gentleman, such as yourself. Living there all alone. But, if you were my boy… and you'll excuse me for saying it…you wouldn't sleep there a night, not if I had to go there myself and pull the big alarm bell that's on that roof!

NARRATOR
Oh, you don't have to be concerned about me. I've got so much research for a major study in Mathematical Science…too much to be disturbed by mysterious goings-on. If you really want a mystery, you should try reading, Talleyrand's "Harmonical Progression, Permutations and Combinations, and Elliptic Functions!"

WOMAN
I hope you're right. I'll have Johnny bring your parcels up to the house as soon as possible. Do you have furniture? If not, I'll tell him to bring the wagon round and stock up on some odds and ends I have out in the barn.

NARRATOR
I'm staying mostly in the grand dining room. I can set up a table and bed there and work when I want. The rest of the house doesn't much matter to me.

WOMAN
Now, you shouldn't be afraid if you hear noises in the night. Ghosts are sometimes everything and anything *but* ghosts.

NARRATOR
Ghosts!

WOMAN
I mean, they often just turn out to be rats and mice and creaky doors and loose slates and open, broken windows letting the wind whistle in…it's an old house, it's got lots of things wrong

with it, even if you can't see them.

(MUSIC)

NARRATOR

"So, despite the warning and local wives' tales, all of which, since I, a modern man, a scientist, I quickly dismiss as primitive superstitions...I've now settled into the place and I've just finished a quick supper I made from bread and butter and chicken broth...Food is my least concern. I must work now, expecting I'll stay up most of the night on my facts and figures. But, I don't need to worry about waking at any certain time. I can do as I like here. This is *my* place, now. Feels good to be sitting in front of *my* fireplace...the place is so quiet, I can hear a pin drop.

(DISTANT NOISE)

"What? So soon? Don't tell me that the rats have already begun their invasion?

(NOISE AGAIN)

"Hmmm...maybe, they're afraid that *I'm* the invader in *their* house? Here I am lighting up a fire and cooking food...where *they've* lived for years in darkness.

(NOISES)

"Busy little guys, aren't they? Sounds like they're in the walls...or upstairs running about. Well, I won't let them bother me. Go on and play and do those things rodents are apt to do. Although...I should take the lamp here and just make a quick round of the place. Can't hurt, can it? Hmmm...I hadn't really looked at the place before now...The carving of the oak on the panels of the wainscot is really fine. And on and round the doors and windows... great craftsmanship. These old pictures on the walls...coated in dust...I wonder if any of them are valuable?" Aha! I see you over there, Mister Rat...I can see your little, red, beady eyes staring at me. Sitting on my chair, are you? Go on! Get out! "Now, what's this? Look at him run up that rope...that must be the rope to that great alarm bell on the roof...well, we'll leave that be for now. Don't want to frighten the neighbors. Time for tea.

(MUSIC)

(Snoring, awakens) Hmmph! "Must have dozed off...too many numbers swimming before my eyes, I suppose. I should get new eye glasses. Of course, calculating by lamp light isn't the way to...oh, the fire's gone down.... what! Am I seeing things? No...I do see it...those red, beady eyes again...staring at me, sitting on my chair again, are you?" Get out! Out of here, I say! Oh, so you're not afraid? Go ahead, bare your teeth at me...think I'm afraid of you?

(SMASH)

Take that! Oh...missed you, did I?

(RAT SQUEAKING)

Yeah, you'd better run! Go on up that rope and hide, you little...

(CLOCK STRIKES)

"Damn, is it morning already? Well, I don't have to get up...this is *my* house now...I can go back to sleep if I want to. Then, I'll eat breakfast. Do some work. And, go for a walk into town..."

(MUSIC)

WOMAN
How are things up at the house? I must say, you're looking pale today. Getting enough sleep? Keeping late hours and too hard work on the brain isn't good for any man! Any...*strange* things going on up there?

NARRATOR
No, no ghosts, I'm afraid. But, the damned rats...they're having a field day. It's like a circus at times. They have free reign of the whole house. There is one wicked-looking old devil that sits up on my chair by the fire, and won't go till I take the poker to him... and then he runs up the rope of the alarm bell and must have some hole in the wall up near the ceiling...I can't see where, it's so dark.

WOMAN
Mercy on us! An old devil, and sitting on the chair by the fireside! Take care, sir! Take care! An old devil, indeed. You shouldn't jest about such things.

NARRATOR

What do you mean?

WOMAN

An old devil? More likely, *the* old devil, himself.

NARRATOR

Ha!

WOMAN

Don't laugh. You young folks think it easy to laugh at things that makes older ones shudder. Never mind, sir! Never mind! Please God, you'll laugh all the time. I hope you never stop laughing.

NARRATOR

I'm sorry. Forgive me. Don't think I'm rude... but the idea was too much for me... that the old devil *himself* was on the chair last night!

(MUSIC, SQUEAKING,
SCRATCHING, THUMPING IN WALLS)

"Well, you've started early tonight. You might have, at least, let me smoke my pipe by the fire in peace. Ah...there they are, the little buggers. All those beady, little red eyes...I should plug that hole down by the floor.
Why? They'll only find another way in. This is *their* house, after all. The noise is getting louder, though. More of them are coming down here into the room lately...they're getting brazen, alright. Other than the noise, they don't bother me. But, one did jump up on my table before...just as I was eating my sandwich. I shooed him away.

(SILENCE)

"But, that is getting to be a bit too much. Wait a second...wait...now, it's stopped. Just stopped. I wonder...oh Jesus! What...is that? Sitting on my chair...that's the biggest rat I've ever seen! It's the size of a small dog. Well, we'll see about that! Here, Mr.Rat, let's see how you like a textbook beaned off your head!

(CRASH)

"Missed. And, he didn't move a muscle. Alright, I'll just bash him with the poker! Damn! Up the rope again...
(RATS NOISE AGAIN)

"And now...the noises begin again...strange. Well, I know...I'll put an extra lamp in that corner...to keep it nice and bright. And, I'll stack a lot of books here as ammunition the next time any of them appear. And, in the morning, I'll see where that rope leads to up there... maybe I can buy some mouse traps...although, that monster was so big...I'd need a fox trap. But, I'm not going to let vermin run me out. I paid for three months rent. Ah, and I'll just tie the bell rope high up in a knot. Won't my little friend be surprised when he tries to reach it next time! Now, back to my studies...
(MUSIC, CLOCK STRIKES)

"It's been there for over an hour now...the big rat...sitting in the big chair staring at me. I've thrown five, six books at it...it jumps aside and returns again. But, this one...
(LOUD SQUEAK)

Got ya, ya blasted rodent! Oh, bare your teeth at me again...go on, I dare you...I oughta crush you with this here poker! What? Can't get up the rope again? Ha! Go on...where to now? Oh...so you've got another hiding place...in that hole behind the table, is it? Right under the old painting, is it? I'll remember that in the morning. I won't forget. So, let's see...what book is it that finally got you? Oh...The Bible my mother gave me! What an odd... coincidence.
(MUSIC)

WOMAN
The rat always went up the rope of the alarm bell?

NARRATOR
Well, yes...until I tied it in a knot.

WOMAN
I suppose you don't know what that rope is, then?

NARRATOR
No. What do you mean?

WOMAN

Now, don't laugh...but, as local legend will have it...it is the very rope which the hangman used for all the victims of the Judge's death sentences. The Judge would ring that bell on his roof every time he sent a man to death. Letting the rest of the town know...just in case they were even thinking of committing a crime. Not that he cared much if they were innocent or not...he'd sooner hang a poor boy who stole a loaf of bread as he would hang a murderer. They say, it rang quite a lot in the old days.

NARRATOR

Well, now...is that so?

WOMAN

But, pay no mind to the local legend. If ever you find yourself in any trouble...you ring that bell, you hear?
(MUSIC, THUNDER STORM OUTSIDE, CLOCK STRIKES, RATS NOISE)

NARRATOR

(Stretches) Ohhhh! "I've been sitting here for...how long has it been? Must be ten o'clock. Ah, the boys are still at it in the walls...up and down the stairs. Getting used to it actually. I won't call them companions, exactly. They're hardly pets. But, I'm getting used to them. The only time I don't hear them is when...that big one shows up. Listen to that storm out there. I'm sure this place must have some leaks in the roof. Well...so that rope there...the hangman's rope...really? If so, how many necks has it been around the second before death? And, who put it here? The old judge himself? That's a morbid thing to do. To keep it there as a reminder of all the men he sent to the gallows? I wonder...did he do that for some moralistic, philosophical reason...or, did he just get a big kick out of it reminding him that he ordered men to their deaths? And, frequently, so I've heard. Look at that! The rope is moving, swaying...the big rat...he's coming down the rope! All the while...glaring at me. Well, now, what do *you* want? What are *you* staring at...across the room? What? That old dusty portrait? Yes. But, why? What about it? I can barely see it under all the dust. Let me find a rag to...
(MUSIC)

"Well, I'll be damned…that must be the Judge himself. Dressed in his red robe with the fur collar. Look at that evil, crafty face…that hooked nose, like a bird of prey. And his skin the color of death. Eyes, have you ever seen such eyes? Well, actually, now that I think of it…yes! They resemble…they resemble the eyes of that big old rat! Sitting right over there watching me. Alright…now, I'm frightened. Why? The Judge…in the picture…he's sitting in that same chair where the rat is at this very moment! Yes. There's the fireplace behind him…and there's the bell rope! Look at me, I'm trembling now. Haven't felt like this before, but…no, there's something evil at work here. I can feel it.

(THUNDER CLAP)

Aaaaah! "This won't do! If I go on like this, I'll have to be put away in an asylum. This must stop! My nerves…my imagination…they're getting the best of me. What I need is a good stiff glass of brandy! I've got a bottle of it here somewhere…

(MUSIC, STORM, WIND)

"Listen to that wind howl…everything silent in here again. The fire's almost out. Glowing red now.

(SQUEAKING)

(Drunk) "Ah, the rope is swinging again. Why, if it isn't Mr.Rat? What are you doing? Gnawing at the rope? Cutting it in half? Why, good sir? Oh…my head. Too much brandy, I'm afraid. Well, it seems you've cut the rope down. Now, it's out of my reach…I won't be able to ring it now… for… assistance." So, that's what you're up to, is it? Take that!

(CRASH)

Got away, you dirty little bastard? Go hide in the shadows. That's all you're good for. If I wasn't so drunk…I'd…I'd…hey, now…that's odd. The picture… the Judge's portrait…am I going blind, or what? That's funny, I know I'm a bit tipsy, but…but…oh my God! What's happened to the Judge in the painting? The chair, it's empty…the Judge is gone! The Judge is gone…the Judge is gone…well, that isn't exactly correct… because …there you are! In the flesh! Sitting there in the chair with your red robe and the fur collar…staring at me… those glowing eyes of yours.

(MUSIC BUILDS)

What do you want with me, you bloody murdering bastard?
(THUNDER, WINDOWS BREAK,
WIND HOWLS)

Don't you point at me!

(CLOCK STRIKES MIDNIGHT)

Don't...you....what are you smiling at? Pointing at me...
pointing...sit down. Sit back down.   You stay right where you
are...don't come near me...the rope? The rope on the
floor...what do you want with that? Put it back... put it down, I
say...what are you doing? Tying...tying a *noose*? Get away
from me! I'm warning you! You can't get away with this...stop
staring at me...I'll leave! That's what I'll do, I'll leave right now!
"But, I can't leave...I'm paralyzed...frozen here...can't move.
Jesus! He's coming closer! Closer! He's playing with me.
Cat and mouse. Mouse! Ha! That's *me*, now! Did you hear
that, boys? I see you! All of you...staring out of your holes,
every little crack in the wall... watching the show, boys? Are
you having a good time? Jumping up onto the bell rope now,
are you? What's left of it...so many of you. Hundreds of you.
Pulling down on it...

(ROOF BELL RINGS ONCE)

"Well...you've done it now. Do you hear that, Judge? Why are
your eyes glowing like hot coals? Like the... devil, himself?
(BELL RINGING, THUNDER, WIND,
MUSIC)

"Jesus in Heaven...I can feel his icy fingers around my
neck...adjusting the noose. Tightening it...tightening
it...Please God, help me...he's picking me up now...like I'm a
little baby, carrying me...to the chair...standing me upon
it...he's tying the rope to the hanging end of it...the rats,
they're all running off up the rope...no! No! Judge! No! Don't
kick the chair! Please, no... don't kick the...!"
(MUSIC, CROWD NOISE, DOOR POUNDING)

WOMAN

Listen! The bell has stopped ringing…hurry, break down that door, men!

(DOOR BREAKING)

Hello! Hello in there? Look!

(CROWD STARTLED)

I was afraid of this…Dear Lord…the poor boy…I told him, I warned him that too much work, not enough sleep would drive him to…now, look…he's gone and hanged himself…may the Lord forgive him. Everyone stand back. Someone go and tell the Vicar…though, it's too late now for him to do much good. Quickly now, cut the poor boy down from there. Take him out of here…down to my place. That's it…easy now. Let's get out of this damned house as fast as we can. Johnny, grab my table and things….we won't be coming back here. Hey now, what's this? That picture…is that the Judge? I've never seen that before. All clean and new…like the boy fixed it up a bit. Look at that wicked smile on the old man's face, will ya? Smiling like the devil, he is. No, we won't be taking that. Leave it be. It belongs here.

IN THE DARK
By Dan Bianchi
From A Story By Edith Nesbit

Cast – 3m
Running Time – 15min
Synopsis – A man is haunted by his murder victim

(MUSIC)

ROB
"I've just come home from the war, you know. On my way to see my friend, a good friend, Billy Haldane. Nicest guy you'd ever want to meet. Known him since grade school. Funny, always made me laugh. But, a good person. Solid. So, what happens as soon as I open the door…

(DOOR OPENS)

" to his room at Grayson's hotel down on Main Street? I'm greeted by a cold, pale, anemic man… with dull eyes and a limp hand, and pale lips that no longer smile nor chuckle…who utters a welcome without gladness. Living, existing amongst a litter of disordered furniture and personal effects half-packed. Boxes, cases of books, filled and waiting."

BILLY
Hello, Robert. Welcome home. Sorry, I wasn't at the station to greet you, but, as you can see…I'm in the middle of moving and…I can't stand these rooms. There's something strange about them…something very strange. I clear our tomorrow.

ROB
You got the present? The trunk I sent with the fur coat? I know you get cold in the winter. I bought it off a rich guy in Paris. That's real mink, you know. You'll look real spiffy in that, for sure, strutting down Broadway in New York City.

BILLY
Fur coat? Oh yes. Thanks. Yes. I forgot about the fur coat.

ROB

You're still going to New York City, right? We always said we'd get there one day...see all the shows, live it up.

BILLY

New York? Well...

ROB

Come on, put this stuff aside and let's go out to eat. I'm starving.

BILLY

Well, Robert, you see, I'd go out to dinner, but, I'm so busy here. But, I'm awfully glad to see you...so, why don't you go down to the restaurant and bring me back a little something?

ROB

Yeah, sure, Billy...

(MUSIC)

"So, I do just that, trying my best to come to terms as to why my good friend has changed so much from the person I remembered to this mere shell of a man. When I return to his room, I bring back a couple of dinners and we eat by the fireplace by candlelight. The electricity must be shut off since he's leaving. Unless, he doesn't pay his bills. I try to be amusing and he tries to be amused. His haggard eyes watch me all the time...except when he's looking back over his shoulder as if someone is behind him. Peering into the shadows. Until I get tired of talking to the back of his head." Well? What's the matter with you?

BILLY

What do you mean?

ROB

What do I mean? You look terrible. What have you been up to? Drinking and gambling? Bad speculation in the market? If you won't tell me, you'll need to see a psychiatrist. I'm not kidding. You look like a nervous wreck.

BILLY

Thanks for your concern.

ROB

I'm your friend, Billy. Do you think I'd turn a blind eye like some stranger who doesn't care? Something's gone wrong and you've taken to something. Morphine? Is that it? Are you in physical pain? You're brooding over something, is that it? Until you've lost all sense of proportion. Out with it. I'll bet you a dollar it's not so bad as you think it is.

BILLY

If I could tell you...or tell anyone, it wouldn't be so bad as it is. If I could tell anyone, I'd tell you. And even as it is, I've told you more than I've told anyone else.

ROB

Told me? Told me what? Is that it? You're not going to say anything else?

BILLY

You can stay here for the night?

ROB

No. I have to get back to my room at the hotel. I'm expecting letters. "So I leave him, looking like a scared rabbit...standing on the stairs, holding a candle over the banisters to light me down.

(MUSIC)

"Well, I'm up half the night wondering what's happened to Billy, determined to get to the bottom of it, but, when I return to his apartment...he's already gone. Left no address with the landlord. Just rode off in a coach. Well, if that's the way he wants to be, a man has a right to his own troubles. I've got enough of my own to keep me busy.

(MUSIC)

"About a year later , I see Billy again. I'm up in Albany, and he turns up one morning, before breakfast...and he looks even more ghastly than before, like a ghost. His face is gaunt and he's so thin, his clothes look three sizes too big for him. His hands are bony, like bird's claws, trembling. We sit down to breakfast and this time, I decide not to ask questions. Actually, I don't need to…he's here to tell me everything, it seems."

BILLY

I am going to kill myself…

ROB

What?

BILLY

No, don't be alarmed. I won't do it here, or now. I'll do it when I have to…when I can't bear it any longer. And I want someone to know why. I don't want to feel that I'm the only living creature who does know. And I can trust you, can't I?

ROB

Yes.

BILLY

I should like you, if you don't mind, to give me your word, that you won't tell a soul what I'm going to tell you, as long as I'm alive. Afterwards…you can tell whom you please.

ROB

You have my word.

BILLY

Well…this is very difficult to say…The fact is…you remember that sonuvabitch we went to school with… George Visger?

ROB

George Visger…yes, I haven't seen him since I came back. Some one told me he'd gone off to some island on vacation and hadn't returned. Probably preaching his bullshit to the cannibals. Anyhow, he's out of the way, bad luck to him.

BILLY

Yes, he's out of the way. But he's not preaching anything. In point of fact, he's dead.

ROB

Dead? Really?

BILLY

Yes, it's not generally known, but he is.

ROB

What did he die of?

BILLY

You know what a stuck-up ass he always was? Always knew everything. Liked to have heart-to-heart talks with people...he's your *friend*, you can tell him anything...and, somehow, he'd persuade you to open up your heart and then...he'd go and tell someone else everything... including a lot of lies...yes, he told *her*, Louise, a pack of lies.

ROB

Lies? What kind of lies?

BILLY

Well, some things were true, about my...sexual persuasion...you know?

ROB

He said *that?* The old boy was a flaming homosexual himself. Hard to disguise *that*. But, he did love to reveal others like himself to the world...had a perverted joy in it. Forcing them to join him on the firing line. And, he told *her*...about *you*?

BILLY

But, he made lies of them the way he told them to her... you know? And she broke off our engagement. And then, she died. And, we weren't even friends. And, I couldn't see her...before...I couldn't even explain...

ROB

I had no idea...

BILLY

Oh, my God....But, I went to the funeral. *He* was there. They'd asked him to attend since he was such a *good friend* of hers. Mr.Big Shot...you know, he's become a bishop or something.

ROB

Really? I knew he was a minister of some sort...

BILLY

Oh, he went straight up the ladder...making deals, befriending everyone, meeting all the politicians and royalty.

ROB

It suits him. Probably, blackmailing them with everything he knows about their private lives.

BILLY

So, when I went back to my rooms, I was sitting there, thinking. And, what do you know?

(KNOCKS)

He came to my door...Visger.

ROB

He would, that bum. Come to gloat, I guess. I hope you kicked his holy ass down the stairs.

BILLY

No, I didn't. I listened to what he had to say.

VISGER

No doubt it was all for the best, Bill. I didn't really know for certain about you...but, I had guessed it. So, I told her. I told Louise. Because, she *should* know, after all.

BILLY

He'd only guessed. He'd guessed right, damn him. What right had he to guess right?

VISGER

I'm heartily sorry she took her own life, but...In the end, it was all for the best...you have to admit it...you couldn't fool her forever, you know? How might it be...married to a woman? She might have loved you, Billy, but, let's face it...you could not have *truly* loved her. It's not fair. Not that there aren't thousands of us in that situation. Living lies. It's not right. To either the man or the woman. Besides, you know... there's madness in your family.

ROB

Madness? And is there?

BILLY

If there is, I didn't know about it. But, somehow, he found that out. And, that was why it was "all for the best."   And then I said, "There wasn't any madness in my family before, but there is now," and I got hold of his throat. I am not sure whether I meant to kill him... Anyhow, I *did* kill him. So...what do you say to *that*, Robert?

ROB

"I say nothing. It is not easy to think at once of the tactful and suitable thing to say, when your oldest friend tells you that he is a murderer."

BILLY

When I could get my hands off of his throat...they felt glued to it... as if an electrical charge held me fast to him...he fell in a lump on the rug. And I saw what I'd done. How is it that murderers ever get found out?

ROB

They're careless, I suppose...they lose their nerve.

BILLY

I didn't. I never was calmer. I sat down in the big chair and looked at him, and thought it all out. He was just leaving for that island...I knew that. He'd said goodbye to everyone. He'd told me that. There was no blood to get rid of...just a touch at the corner of his slack mouth.   It was all as plain as day. There was nothing to get rid of, but, the man. The corpse. No weapon, no blood...and I got rid of him all right.

ROB

How? You didn't...cut him up?

BILLY

No, no, that's where I draw the line.

ROB

Oh, I see. Well, where is it? His body, I mean? It's not that I doubt your word, but....

BILLY

No, no. As long as you don't know where the body is, don't you see, I'm all right. Even if you could prove that I've said all this...which you can't...it's only the wanderings of my poor unhinged brain. Understand? Madness in the family. See?

ROB

"I do see. And I'm sorry for Billy. I don't really believe that he's killed Visger. He's not the sort of man who kills people." Yes, I see. Now look here. Let's go away together, you and I...we'll travel a bit and see the world, and forget all about that asshole, Visger.

BILLY

Really? Why, that's...so, you *do* understand? You don't hate me? You don't want to run away from me?

ROB

Don't be ridiculous.

BILLY

I wish I'd told you before...you know, when you came and I was packing all my stuff. But, it's too late now.

ROB

Too late? Not at all. Let's pack our bags and be off tonight...out into the unknown, right?

BILLY

Hold on...when you've heard what's been happening to me, you won't be so keen to go traveling about with me.

ROB

What? There's more?

BILLY

Well, I've told you what happened to him. What happened to me is quite different. Did I tell you what his last words were? Just

when I was coming at him. Before I'd got his throat, you know.
He said...

VISGER (ECHO)

Look out.! You'll never to able to get rid of the body... Besides,
anger's sinful!

BILLY

You know that way he had, looking into your eyes, soulfully, as
if he was so interested in you, only you. Even up until that last
second. Lately, I got to thinking of that. But, I didn't think of it
for a year. Because I did get rid of his body all right. And, then,
I was sitting in that comfortable chair, and I thought, "Hey, it
must be about a year now, since that night." and I pulled out
my calendar ...and sure enough it was a year, to the day. And
then I remembered what he'd said. And, I said to myself, "Not
much trouble about getting rid of your body, you obnoxious
fool." And then I looked at the rug and... (Screams)
Aaaahhhh!

ROB

What, Billy? What?

BILLY

I can't tell you...no, I can't.

ROB

Here...here's a shot of whiskey. Down it...pull yourself
together...You must tell me everything. Free your mind...

BILLY

Where was I?

ROB

You were looking at your calendar...and then the rug...what did
you see? What was it?

BILLY

Nothing much...oh, nothing much...only that I glanced at the
rug...and there he was...the man I'd killed a year before.

ROB

Well…

BILLY

Don't try to explain, or I shall lose my temper. The door was shut. The windows were shut. He hadn't been there a minute before. And he was there, then. That's all.

ROB

Hallucination?

BILLY

Exactly what I thought. But, I touched it. It was quite real. Heavy, you know, and harder than live people are somehow, to the touch…more like a stone thing covered with skin…and the arms like a marble statue.

ROB

There are hallucinations of touch, too…

BILLY

Exactly what I thought.   But there are limits, you know… limits. So, then I thought someone had got him out of where he'd been hiding…the real him…and stuck him there to frighten me…while my back was turned, and I went to the place where I'd hidden him, and he was still there! Just as I'd left him. Only…it was a year ago. There are *two* of him there now.

ROB

Oh, Billy…this is turning into a comedy. *Two* of him? Where did the other one come from? *Two* bodies? Really now..

BILLY

Yes, it is amusing. I find it so myself. Especially in the night when I wake up and think of it. I hope I don't die in the dark, Robert. That's one of the reasons why I think I shall have to kill myself. I could be sure then of not dying in the dark.

ROB

Is that all?

BILLY

No, that's not all. He's come back to haunt me again.

ROB

Visger is back?

BILLY

On the train, it was. I'd been asleep. The only passenger in the car. When I woke up, there he was lying on the seat opposite me. Looked just the same. I threw him out while going through a tunnel. No one saw me, I'm sure. But, if I see him again, I'm going out myself. I can't stand it. It's too much. I'd sooner go. Whatever the next world's like, there aren't things in it like that. We leave them here, in graves and boxes and... You think I'm mad. But I'm not. You can't help me...no one can help me. He knew, you see. He said I shouldn't be able to get rid of the body. And, I can't get rid of it. I can't. I can't. He knew. He always did know things that he couldn't know. But, I'll cut his game short. After all, I've got the ace of trumps, and I'll play it on his next trick. I give you my word of honor, Robert, that I'm not mad.

ROB

I don't think you're mad, Billy. But I do think your nerves are very much upset. Mine are a bit, too. Do you know why I went off to war? It was because of you and her. I couldn't stay and see it, though, I wished for your happiness and all that...you know I did. And when I came back, when I heard about her...death and...

BILLY

You were in love with her?

ROB

Not *her*, Billy...not her.

BILLY

What? You mean...? Robert...I...I...didn't know.

ROB

Look, that's all in the past. We've got the future to live for. Let's go through all this together, alright? You won't keep seeing things if you've got me to talk to.

BILLY

She liked you...

ROB

I know.

BILLY

But, do you suppose...Visger knew...about you...and about me...and told her?

ROB

It could be. In fact, I'd bet that's what happened.

BILLY

I guess I should feel some sort of vindication for killing him.

ROB

Well, things will be different now. You'll see.

(MUSIC)

"So, we leave for Europe. I'm glad now that Billy has confided in me...and that I've done the same with him. Things don't turn romantic between us. But, we become closer than ever. I can't believe that he's gone mad, not permanently. After a month, the madness seems to pass away, and we find ourselves having a good time on the French Riviera. We never speak of Visger. I think he's forgotten all about him. I think I understand how his mind, over-strained by sorrow and anger, had fixed on the man he hated, and woven a nightmare web of horror round that detestable personality. But, enough of that. We're full of ourselves. Sight seeing, getting drunk, living it up...Going over our trip to Venice..."

BILLY

I wonder if we can travel the canals in a gondola by moonlight?

ROB

Why not? Oh, my head. Well, I think we've had enough wine for tonight. It's time for bed. We've got a big day tomorrow. If we can even wake up on time...

BILLY

Robert...I want to tell you something. I've left everything to you, my friend. In my will. I know I can trust you to see to everything.

ROB

Well, of course. But, if you don't mind, we'll talk about it in the morning.

BILLY

You've been such a good friend...

ROB

Come on now, go to sleep. Get in your bed.

BILLY

Can you get me a glass of water?

ROB

What? You're like a child. Can't get it yourself?

BILLY

No, I don't want to walk down the stairs in the dark. I might...I might step on something...or walk into something that wasn't there before...

ROB

What the hell are you talking about? Walk into something? What, your grandmother? Hey, you're trembling. What's wrong? You're looking pale. Do you have a fever? What's this here? Oh...

BILLY

What?

ROB

On the sheet...this dark area here...I thought it was blood. But, it's red stitching on the white sheet...initials G.V.

BILLY

G....V....?

ROB

Grande Vigne Hotel, of course. I guess they don't want people stealing the sheets. Ok, I'll go get you some water.

BILLY

No, I don't want to stay alone in the dark.

ROB

All right then, come along. "After all this time and trouble, it's plain to me, he isn't cured at all. What a great disappointment. So, we go downstairs as quietly as we can, and get a carafe of water from the kitchen. He takes hold of my arm, at first, and, then, he takes the candle away from me, and goes very slowly, shading the light with his hand... and looking very carefully all about, as though he expects to see something that he wants very desperately *not* to see. And, of course, I know what that something is. I don't like this. Not at all. Looking over his shoulder every now and then, just as he did that first evening after I came back from the war. It's getting on my nerves. I can hardly find the way back to our room. And, when we get there, I more than half-expect to see what *he* expects to see...lying there on the rug. But, of course, there is nothing. I blow out the light and tighten my blankets round me...we're in separate beds, of course."

BILLY

You've got all the blankets.

ROB

No, I haven't.

BILLY

I can't find mine...And I'm cold. I'm. . . For God's sake, light the candle. Light it. Light it. Something horrible...

ROB

What now? I can't find the matches.

BILLY

Light the candle, light the candle...If you don't, he'll come to me. It is so easy to come at any one in the dark. Oh Robert, light the candle, for the love of God! I can't die in the dark.

ROB

I'm looking for the matches! I don't know where I put them.
And, you're *not* going to die. Stop saying that. Don't be a fool.
It's all right. I'll get a light in a second.

BILLY

It's cold. It's cold. It's cold…

ROB

"Just like that, he says it, three times. And then…"
(BILLY SCREAMS)

What is it? Billy! For God's sake, stop screaming. You'll have
the whole building awake…What is it?…Billy?

BILLY

(Pause) It's Visger…

ROB

Nonsense. Where? Ah, I've found the matches…hold on…
(STRIKES MATCH)

BILLY

Here! Here he is, beside me. In the bed.

ROB

"I light the candle and go across to him. He's crushed in a heap
at the edge of the bed. Stretched on the bed beyond him is a
dead man, white and very cold. And, now I look back to
Billy…and he's dead, as well. He's died in the dark, just as he
had feared.
(MUSIC)

"Now, I know what has happened. It's all so simple. In our
drunken stupor, we've come to the wrong room. The man the
room belongs to is there, on the bed…in the dark…lying there
all day, dead from a heart attack. A French perfume salesman.
A mere mistake and overwhelming fear has caused the death of
my friend.
(SHIP HORN, MUSIC)

"When I return home…I make cautious enquiries. Months

earlier, the body of a man had been found in the train tunnel...a haberdasher named Simmons, who had committed suicide by taking cyanide on the train. He still had the bottle clenched in his hand. Billy had tossed a dead man off the train that day, not a ghost. At last, I come to the items Billy left to me in his will. Boxes. One of them is the big trunk, an expensive Louis Vuitton ...metal lined... in which I had sent him the fur coat from Paris. Had he never even opened it? Well, he must have...because now... the trunk is bolted shut. I haven't the key. It takes some time to open it. Inside is the coat, no? No. The bodies of two men. That's right, two. One is identified, after some trouble, as that of an office worker subject to fits. The cause of his death, it seems. Only Billy didn't know that, of course. Why or how he got here, I don't know. The other body is, indeed, George Visger's. Explain it as you like. This is all I know. I have not yet found the explanation that can satisfy me."

GREEN TEA
By Dan Bianchi
From A Story By Sheridan Le Fanu

Cast – 3m, 1w
Running Time – 15 min
Synopsis – A priest is haunted by a demon monkey

(MUSIC)

MARY
My poor Uncle...I'm so worried about him. He's been acting so strange lately. Why, in the very act of relating a sermon to his congregation... I saw him break down in tears. A look of fright on his face. Pale as death. Then, he started muttering prayers to himself...as if the rest of us weren't even there. After that, he didn't even conclude the service... he just rushed into the vestry and slammed the door behind him. His odd behavior may be due to stress...he may be overwrought, worried.

HESSEL
Tell me more about the way he acts at church services.

MARY
Well, while he's at the pulpit, he has a way of looking... squinting...at the carpet. As if there is something there... his eyes following it as it moves. But, of course, there is nothing there. I've seen him do that a few times.

HESSEL
Well, I've spoken to your Uncle.

MARY
You have?

HESSEL
Yes, and I like him very much. The Pastor is a fine man. Well educated, well spoken. Well traveled, too.

MARY
And, good natured. He's been a tremendous help in building a new school in our community.

HESSEL

He's unmarried.

MARY

Yes, that's true.

HESSEL

He wanted to be a writer, but, has since, given up that notion. Oh, and he drinks very little coffee, but, he does love a good strong cup of green tea every night.

MARY

Well, he claims that he can't live without it.

HESSEL

As for his parents, his father died ten years ago. But, and this is very confidential...

MARY

Of course...

HESSEL

He purports to have seen his father's ghost.

MARY

He told you that? I must say, you've gotten more out of him in one visit than I have in the past five years.

HESSEL

Well...it may interest you to know...Pastor Jennings is just as interested in the spirit world and the supernatural, than he is in church business.

MARY

I don't understand.

HESSEL

While at his home, his servant had asked me to wait for him in his library. In there, I found several books on arcane and occult topics. In one book...he had written in the margins...notes about opening one's interior sight into the spirit world...and, when in that other world, other things appear...

MARY
Other things?

HESSEL
Things of another life... which are not visible to the material world.

MARY
I had no idea he is interested in such subjects.

HESSEL
Oh, he's very interested. In fact, he believes that *he* , himself, has this internal sight which grants him the ability to see those *things* in the other world. In another note...he wrote. that, within each man there are, at least, two evil spirits. He believes that there are wicked genii who have their own language.

MARY
Genii? Like in Aladdin's lamp?

HESSEL
Oh, I fear much worse than that.

MARY
This is madness.

HESSEL
Indeed, you may be right. I've heard these beliefs before. The asylums are filled with such believers.

MARY
Do you think my Uncle is mad?

HESSEL
He believes that evil spirits associated with man are the usual demons and devils from Hell...but, they also inhabit that *other* world, the world of spirits *between* Heaven and Hell. The Pastor believes...these demons try their best to possess human beings...they hate mankind, naturally, so they wish to destroy him.

MARY

I can't believe that I am hearing this...

HESSEL

It does not get better. Pastor Jennings believes that he, himself, is possessed by such evil which is trying to destroy him...body and soul.

MARY

And, all of this, you read in the margins of a book?

HESSEL

Well, several books...I waited for a long time in that room.

MARY

But, he's a man of God. Isn't he?

HESSEL

Oh, yes, definitely. He believes strongly that his faith shall protect him from evil spirits. He repeatedly scribbled many prayers and intonations to the Lord God throughout the book. Over and over again. Now...while I was examining these writings...it was at that point, Pastor Jennings entered the room. An embarrassing situation.

MARY

What happened?

HESSEL

Nothing much. He apologized for not having the time to meet with me. He had to run to a dying parishioner's bedside. When I had asked, where...he seemed not to know...and left the room.

MARY

Do you think he was lying?

HESSEL

Well...he not only left the room, he left the county. That was last week. His servant said that he had gone to the seaside for reasons of his health and left another priest in charge of church matters. I received this letter today from him...claiming that he's had a nice vacation, a change of air, he's feeling much better and...he wants to see me at his house in Harley Street today at six. He says that he has *something* to tell me.

MARY
That sounds mysterious. It's nearly six now. You *are* going?

HESSEL
Certainly.

MARY
And you *will* tell me everything when you return?

HESSEL
Of course. That's why you're paying me to investigate the situation, isn't it?

(MUSIC)

JENNINGS
It began on the 15th of October, three years ago...I count every day...every day is torment for me. Well, a year before that...I began to formulate a book analyzing religious metaphysics of the ancients. I wrote a great deal. Late at night. I was consumed by the subject matter. Always thinking about it, walking about, talking to myself. Obsessed by it. Addicted to it. And all the while...I became addicted to quite another thing...Tea became my companion. At first, ordinary black tea made in the usual way, not too strong. But, I drank a good deal of it, increasing its strength as I went on. It never affected me in a negative way. But, the taste no longer interested me. So, then, I turned to green tea. I found that it cleared and intensified the power of thought, so, I took it frequently. So, I sat up all through each night sipping on my green tea...as I studied and researched and wrote my book. I had a little kettle on my table heated by a laboratory gas jet. I made tea two or three times between eleven and three o'clock in the morning. Other than that, I'd go into town each day and work in the library for a few hours and meet friends. There was no after-affect that I could detect.

Well...at this time, I met an old bookseller who had just the right edition of a particular book which I needed. He had it at his home up in Springfield. I'd taken a bus there and purchased the book from him, and, near night fall, I returned to my home in Lakeland on the last bus heading north…

(BUS SOUNDS)

So, here I am, the only passenger left on board by the time we reach Lindenhurst. Not far to go now. But, it's getting very dark. And, I observe…for the first time…that, on the floor, under a seat opposite me…what's that? Two small circular reflections…they're reddish color …like glowing red lights. Two inches apart. I blink my eyes. Must be seeing things. We're lumbering along gently, having nearly a mile still to go. The two luminous, red dots…they haven't gone away. With every jerk of the bus over bumps and turns in the road, these circles are affected …they move as if jostled about….oh look! They've just risen to the level of the seat where I am sitting! And, now…they are gone….Oh! Now they are back near the floor again…gone again. Now, up in a corner of another seat. What is this? Are my eyes playing tricks? Well, let's just find out. So, I keep my gaze fixed upon them…while I edge myself quietly towards these tiny red discs.

The bus is nearly pitch black. There are no passing lights out here in the country. But, there are those red circles and, like myself, they shift back and forth as if rocked by the bus's movement. Ah, I see…an outline now…getting more distinct, silhouetted in a very dim light cast from the driver's dashboard. And, what is this? It appears to be…a small black *monkey*, pushing its face forward to meet mine. Those red discs…are its eyes, and I now dimly see… its teeth grinning at me.

I don't know if I should be afraid. It might be getting ready to spring at me. Could one of the passengers have forgotten this ugly pet? Well…I poke my umbrella at it. It doesn't move. In fact…I must be going insane…the umbrella passes right *through* the thing!

Now, I am afraid, deathly afraid! I am definitely seeing things, now. See! Now, it skips backward…back into the corner. Open the window! I need fresh air! That's it, clear your brain…

(BUS STOPS, DOOR OPENS)

                              DRIVER
Lakeland. Last stop.

                             JENNINGS
I disembark, the bus drives off

                                          (BUS DRIVES OFF)

And I am alone on the road. The first question…has the
monkey followed me? I don't see it. I don't hear it. That's that.
Yes, it must have been a pet animal somehow left behind on
the bus. Ha! Won't the poor driver be in for a shock! Now,
let's get home…

                                                    (MUSIC)
There's my house, hiding behind a wall of hedges, down a little
dirt path. But, unfortunately…I am not alone in my journey.
The monkey is back… on all fours, walking or creeping, close
beside me. I stop to look down at it. There's not light enough
to see it much more than in outline. Not enough reflective light
to see its eyes. It's observing me, as well. I do hope it's not a
lost animal seeking a new master. As I turn, *it* turns the same
way…as I walk quickly, it does the same. It's so quiet out
here, deserted. And, dark. This *thing*…is it even real? Can it
be some spectral illusion I've read about? Or, something
brought on by brain disease? Perhaps, it's nothing serious. A
temporary condition brought on by little sleep…and a poor
diet…and nervous dyspepsia. If so, it can be corrected. What
am I saying? I don't believe a word of it. Not one word of it.
The fact of the matter is…I am possessed by a satanic entity.

                                    (LOCK OPENS, DOOR OPENS)

Well, home, at last. And…the monkey is still with me…rushed
right past me. Ignore it. That's what I'll do. Drink no tea
tonight. Just cigars, some brandy and water. Try to force
yourself to think other thoughts. Something frivolous,
perhaps. Maybe, I can become inebriated enough to blot out
everything. The monkey is sitting, squatting on the dining
room table. Staring at me.

                                                    (MUSIC)

That was only the first night…three years ago. For the first
year, the monkey never leaves me. That small, black monkey.
Always sullen. Sickly looking. A malignant air about it.

Intense malice. Yes. Always watching. But, only that. Its eyes are never off me. However, at weeks at a time...it disappears. Goes away. I don't know why. Beyond that, the oddest thing about it...not only does its eyes glow red...but, I've noticed, in the dark...there is a halo around the monkey, a reddish halo.

Now, whenever it returns from wherever it's been...it's becoming more agitated. More furious, advancing towards me, grinning and shaking, its paws clenched, and, at the same time...I'm startling to see...flames now burning in the fireplace. I haven't ignited the fire, certainly. I can't sleep in the room when that happens. The monkey gets angry, trembling in rage...it races to the fire and springs up the chimney and it's gone.

The first time it happened, I thought I was, at last, free from this horror. A day passes, a week...another week. Another. I am a new man. I get on my knees and thank God. A whole month passes...before *it* is back again.
It's been with me, ever since.

(MUSIC)

HESSEL
Is it here now?

JENNINGS
No. It has been absent exactly fifteen days. Sometimes, it disappears for nearly two months. Once, for three months. But, I get no peace any more during such intervals. I know it will be back. It can return at any minute.

HESSEL
Is its return accompanied by any peculiar manifestation?

JENNINGS
Nothing...no puffs of smoke, no lightning, no explosions. It is simply with me again. On lifting my eyes from a book, or turning my head, I see it, as usual, looking at me, and, then, it remains, as before, for its appointed time. Funny, I have never told all this to a living soul before now. I...I'm at the end...of my rope. I...don't know what to do.

HESSEL

You don't look well. Shall I come back in the morning?

JENNINGS

No, if you don't mind hearing it all now. I've gotten this far...I don't want to repeat it. When I speak to physicians ...I don't tell them everything, but, well, what do they know about such things? But, you...you do know... don't you? I can tell that you do. Do you think it is just a figment of my imagination, the product of a diseased mind? Or...is it real?

HESSEL

I must know more, before I make any conclusion...

JENNINGS

Very well. In any case, one way or another, I feel as if I am being drawn closer to Hell. May God Almighty help me!

HESSEL

This...monkey...has its aggressiveness increased in time?

JENNINGS

Yes! Its malice toward me...yes, aggressive. It's determined to unnerve me every chance it gets. In the church, at my reading desk, in the pulpit, offering communion. When I read to the congregation, it springs up on my book and squats there. I can't even read the page. More than once, it's done that. Well...awhile ago, I ran away. To the city. I thought, if I could bury myself amidst crowds of people, the monkey would leave me alone. And, it seemed to work. For nearly three months. Once again, I begin to think I am safe. I return to my town. I long to get back to my duty as Pastor and, my replacement, Father Carmichael, is eager to return to his own home.

My first night back...It's a beautiful evening, everything looks serene and cheerful, and I am delighted. I look out of my window and see the spire of my church among the trees...a beautiful sight. I sit on a fence and stare up the hill to the church where I shall deliver my next sermon tomorrow morning and...there, sitting beside me, is the monkey. I feel faint. Wild feelings spin inside me, despair and horror. I close my eyes and pray. Will this persecution never end, Lord?

As I say my prayers, even in meditation, it desperately attempts to interrupt me. How? It's an immaterial phantom, right? How can it affect me? It springs on a table...on the back of a chair...down the chimney... swinging, rocking its body, its head staring at me all the time. As if, hypnotizing me with its motion. Back and forth, back and forth. To a point where I feel I am losing control of my mind. It comes closer, closer...closer. Even with my eyes closed, I see it. (Sobs) It's no use. Prayer does not work against it. What do I do now?

HESSEL
Don't despair, my friend.

JENNINGS
Despair? You haven't even heard the rest of my story, yet. About a year ago...it began to speak to me.

HESSEL
Speak! How do you mean...speak as a man does?

JENNINGS
Yes... speak in words and consecutive sentences, with perfect coherence and articulation... but, there is something even stranger. Its tone is not like the tone of a human voice. I don't hear it through my ears only...it comes like a singing through my head. This new power it has...well, it will cause the end of me for sure. It won't let me pray, it interrupts me with dreadful blasphemies. Saying things you can't imagine.

HESSEL
This thing has no direct power to hurt you unless you allow it to happen. Even God gives you free will to choose your path. Its access to your senses depends mainly upon your physical condition. We are all men. We are the same. In your case, your physical condition needs repair. You must enter upon a new course in life. Be encouraged. We must consider a new path for you to take.

JENNINGS
Do you think so? Really think so? Oh, that is encouraging to

hear that from another human being. Still, I don't know. It's gaining such an influence over me...it orders me about, it is such a tyrant, and I'm growing so helpless. May God deliver me!

HESSEL
It orders you about? Of course, you mean by speech?

JENNINGS
Yes, yes! It is always urging me to commit crimes, to injure others, or myself. It's getting worse. Now, do you see how urgently I need help? Last week, when I was in Port Jefferson, I went out one day with my niece and her friends for a walk...well, my persecutor, that damned beast...I tell you, it was with me at the time. There I am, lagging behind the rest... walking near the shore along the cliffs. We come to a precipice...about a hundred feet high...and I'm staring down at the rocks, the surf crashing against the rocks...and that brute...it's taunting me, telling me to...

VOICE (ECHO)
Throw yourself off the cliff! Throw yourself down onto those rocks!

JENNINGS
I struggle, I fight, I squirm...I must not allow this thing to....

VOICE (ECHO)
Throw yourself off the cliff...now!

JENNINGS
I cannot allow my poor niece to witness such a terrible thing...so, I excuse myself from the others and hurry away. The poor girl has no idea why I am acting this way. She looks so alarmed. I must look frightful. But, she does not leave my side. And, that alone, saves me from a horrible fate. Still, I fear, I am now a slave of Satan.

HESSEL
You were preserved, nevertheless. It was the act of God. You are in His hands and in the power of no other being... be therefore confident for the future. Let's get some light in here.

Make the room a bit more cheerful, no? Think positively. You now know that God is on your side. You must work to repair your physical condition while He shall take care of your spiritual strengthening. Together, you can conquer your fears. You have already shown signs of getting stronger, haven't you? By refusing to follow the commands of that hellish voice within you? God sent your niece to help you, but, *you* did it, my friend. If not, you would not be here.

JENNINGS

That's true. Yes.

HESSEL

Now, if this...*monkey*...should return, at any time, send for me. Have your servant stay near you all night. I shall be back tomorrow. I'll have to think about our next step to take.

(MUSIC)

JENNINGS (ECHO)

"Dear Dr. Hessel...It is here. You had not been an hour gone when it returned. It is speaking. It knows all that has happened. It knows every thing...it knows you, and is frantic and atrocious. It's screaming bloody hatred. I send you this. It knows every word I have written...I write. I am confused. Incoherent now. Interrupted, disturbed. Ever yours, sincerely yours, Robert Lynder Jennings."

(MUSIC)

HESSEL

I don't need to tell you what happened when I arrived at his house.

MARY

Please...

HESSEL

The servant was in tears. There were men there...police. I went upstairs to his room. and...he had done away with himself. I won't describe what I saw...

MARY

It's alright. I want to know.

HESSEL

Very well. He had cut his throat with his razor. It was a frightful gash.

MARY

Dear God...

HESSEL

They had laid him on the bed, and composed his limbs. There's a pool of blood by the window...so, I assume that's where it occurred. There's nothing else I can do, so, I find the servant, Jonathan...and question him before the police do.

JONATHAN

I stayed close to Pastor Jennings, all night, as instructed. Every hour, I'd bring him a fresh cup of green tea.
(CLOCK STRIKES, MUMBLING)

Around three o'clock...I hear him talking to himself in his room. I listen at the door. It's silent. So, I look in upon him...

(DOOR CREAKS)

And there he is...lying, half dressed, in his bed, the sheets and blankets thrown everywhere...leaning on his side staring at something. "Do you need anything, Sir?"

JENNINGS

No. Yes...more green tea.

JONATHAN

But, I know, I can feel that something is not right. I wait another half hour or so and go to his door again with the tea. Silence. I open the door a little. The lights are off in his room. By the hall light, I can see him sitting in his chair. Now, he's fully dressed again. I think to myself, why is he dressed and sitting in the dark like that? He turns and looks at me. Again, I ask, "Do you need help, Sir?"

JENNINGS

No.

HESSEL
Had you heard any other voices? Any loud cursing?

JONATHAN
No, Sir.

HESSEL
Then, what happens?

JONATHAN
So, I say, "Shouldn't you go to bed, Mr.Jennings? It's almost five o'clock in the morning." He just says...

JENNINGS
Very well, Jonathan, good night.

JONATHAN
So, I go and in less than an hour, I look in on him again... and he says...

JENNINGS
Do not to disturb me again.

JONATHAN
And, then, he locks the door.

(DOOR LOCK)

I lay down and slept for a little. It must have been between six and seven when I went up again. The door was still locked...

(KNOCKS)

No answer. So I didn't want to disturb him. I figured, he's asleep.

(CLOCK STRIKES)

I left him till nine. It was his custom to ring when he wished me to come...

HESSEL
You had no assigned time to wake him daily?

JONATHAN

No. So, I tapped very gently.

(KNOCKS)

No answer. Well, he needed his rest, so, I let him be until eleven. Now, I began to get nervous, you see. He'd never slept this late before.

(KNOCKS, DOOR KNOB RATTLE)

"Sir! Wake up!" Still no answer. So not being able to force the door, I called the stable boy and together we forced it

(DOOR POUNDS, BREAKS)

and found him…well, you saw how it was…shocking, just shocking…Poor Pastor Jennings was very gentle, and very kind. All his people were fond of him. What could have happened to make him want to…?

(MUSIC)

HESSEL

I can tell you, I feel so dejected and agitated myself to have it end this way.   I left that house, hoping I shall never see it again.

MARY

It sounds like a frightful, terrible dream.

HESSEL

Yet, I know it is true. It is the story of the process of a poison, a poison which excites the reaction of spirit and nerve…it paralyzes the tissue that separates those cognitive functions of the senses… the external and the interior. Thus, the mortal and immortal prematurely make acquaintance.

MARY

But, surely…these spectral illusions…

HESSEL

Ah, that is a different story. Your uncle's visions…I've treated fifty-seven such cases through the years. I've not failed in one case…until now. I treated such cases as medical conditions as simple as the common cold. There are cures for such things.

But, I had not even begun to treat your Uncle.   I'm sure I could have cured him perfectly within a year or two. Some cases are very rapidly curable, others extremely tedious. With enough thought and diligence applied to the task, I would have found a cure. A medical cure.

MARY

So, you think that it has nothing to do with supernatural causes?

HESSEL

These so-called *supernatural causes,* I believe, are not actually external causes, but, visions created by the inner being of a person. By various abuses, say, the habitual use of such agents as strong green tea...the fluid within the bodily system traveling from the heart to the brain and back...may become affected...it may disturb the equilibrium. This fluid affects the portions of the brain and nervous system...which, in turn, may create these images and sounds, which appear so real, to the victim himself. It's not long before they start to *see* disembodied spirits, or they even communicate with the dead...or, they are attacked by creatures, or possessed by demons from another world. Are these demons any less potent than if they were actually *real* demons? Soon, the victim begins to think they are out to destroy him...as was the case with your uncle.   If only there was more time.   I have not, I repeat, the slightest doubt that I should have cured Pastor Jennings.

MARY

Poor Uncle...if he could have only held on a bit longer.

HESSEL

Well, I must admit, there was another totally different malady that contributed to his case...when added to his disease, it multiplied its potency. It quickened the danger. Complicated matters.

MARY

What can that be?

HESSEL

I'm afraid he actually succumbed to hereditary suicidal mania.

MARY

Really?

HESSEL

Yes, I'm afraid so. In my research, I learned that it has happened quite often in both sides of your family.

MARY

So...do you think that I am at risk, as well?

HESSEL

I should think not...unless, of course...by any chance, you're not addicted to drinking green tea, are you?

SHADOWS ON THE WALL
By Dan Bianchi
From A Story By Mary E. Wilkins Freeman

Cast – 1m, 3w
Running Time – 15min
Synopsis – Sisters suspect their brother has killed their other brother

(MUSIC)

CAROLINE
Henry argued with Edward in the study the night before Edward died.

REBECCA
Caroline! Please…

CAROLINE
I think Henry might have controlled his temper, when poor Edward was so near his end.

REBECCA
Of course, he did not *know*…

CAROLINE
Yes. Of course, he did not know it.

EMMA
What do you mean?

CAROLINE
Nobody means anything.

EMMA
Where are you going?

CAROLINE
I have something to see to. Our brother lies dead upstairs and we have a funeral to arrange, or, have you forgotten?

EMMA

Oh.

(DOOR CLOSE)

Rebecca, did Henry argue with him?

REBECCA

Well, they were talking very loud.

EMMA

Did you...hear anything?

REBECCA

I was just across the hall in the south parlor, and that door was open and this door ajar...I couldn't help hearing...

EMMA

Everything?

REBECCA

Most of it.

EMMA

What was it?

REBECCA

The old story.

EMMA

I suppose Henry was angry, as he always was, because Edward was living on here for nothing, when he had wasted all the money father left him.

REBECCA

Well...

EMMA

I know how he felt. It must have looked to him as if Edward was living at his expense, but he wasn't.

REBECCA

No, he wasn't.

EMMA

And Edward had a right here according to the terms of father's will, and Henry ought to have remembered it.

REBECCA

Yes, he ought.

EMMA

Did he say hard things?

REBECCA

Pretty hard, from what I heard.

EMMA

What?

REBECCA

I heard him tell Edward that he had no business here at all, and he thought he had better go away.

EMMA

What did Edward say?

REBECCA

That he would stay here as long as he lived and afterward, too, if he had a mind to, and he would like to see Henry get him out.. and then...

EMMA

What?

REBECCA

Then he laughed.

EMMA

What did Henry say?

REBECCA

I didn't hear him say anything, but...

EMMA

But what?

REBECCA

I saw him when he came out of this room.

EMMA

He looked angry?

REBECCA

You've seen him when he looked like that.

EMMA

Like that time he killed the cat because she had scratched him?

REBECCA

Yes. Don't remind me!

(DOOR OPENS)

Oh, you're back, Caroline...we were just...I mean...

CAROLINE

Yes, I can imagine. It is time you controlled your nerves, Rebecca.

(DOOR CLOSES)

This door...it should be fixed...it's always sticks so hard. The moisture in the air. The wood expanding. I suppose it will shrink enough after we have the fire going a few days.

EMMA

I think Henry ought to be ashamed of himself for talking as he did to Edward.

CAROLINE

Hush!

EMMA

Nobody can hear with the door shut. I say again I think Henry ought to be ashamed of himself. I shouldn't think he'd ever get over it, having words with poor Edward the very night before he died. Edward was a nicer person than Henry, with all his faults. I never heard him speak a cross word, unless he spoke cross to Henry that last night. Rebecca overheard them.

REBECCA

Not so much cross, as sort of soft, and falsely sweet, and aggravating.

EMMA

What do you really think ailed Edward? I know you said that he had terrible pains in his stomach, and had spasms, but what do you think made him have them?

CAROLINE

Henry called it gastric trouble. You know Edward has always had dyspepsia.

EMMA

Was there any talk of an...examination?

CAROLINE

No! No...don't even say it...

(KNOCK. DOOR OPENS)

EMMA

Henry!

HENRY

Well, hello, ladies. I declare, Emma, you grow younger every year.

CAROLINE

Our thoughts today ought to belong to the one of us who will *never* grow older.

HENRY

Of course, we none of us forget that, but, we have to speak to the living, Caroline, and I have not seen Emma for a long time, and the living are as dear as the dead.

CAROLINE

Not to me.

(DOOR OPEN, CLOSE)

REBECCA

Caroline! Come back...

HENRY

Caroline is completely unstrung. And, Rebecca? She follows her around like a puppy dog.

EMMA

Edward's death was very sudden.

HENRY

Yes, it was very sudden. He was sick only a few hours.

EMMA

What did you call it?

HENRY

Gastric.

EMMA

You did not think of an examination?

HENRY

An autopsy? What for? I'm a doctor. I am perfectly certain as to the cause of his death. Now where are *you* going?

EMMA

I need to...need to get my sewing box...have to sew a headdress for the funeral.

(DOOR CLOSE, MUSIC)

CAROLINE

Don't speak, don't, I won't have it!

EMMA

Alright, I won't. I'll just sit here and sew my black bonnet. Oh, It's no use, I cannot see to sew another stitch until we have a light.

CAROLINE

Rebecca, you had better light a lamp.

REBECCA

Do we really need one?

EMMA

Yes, we do. I can't see to sew another stitch.

REBECCA

Oh...alright.

EMMA

Put it on the table over here.

REBECCA

There? Why there? Do I have to put it there?

EMMA

Well, of course. I am sewing and Caroline is writing letters and this is where we are seated.

CAROLINE

Rebecca? Why are you hesitating? That's it...put it down on the table. What's wrong with you? Why are you shielding your eyes?

REBECCA

I always like to sit in the dark. (Sobs)

CAROLINE

I swear, Rebecca, sometimes you do try a person's very soul...Emma? Emma? Now, what's wrong with you? Why are you staring so hard at that wall?

EMMA

What? Oh, yes...of course...

CAROLINE

I swear...is everyone going insane?

EMMA

Look...what is that?

CAROLINE

What?

EMMA

That strange shadow on the wall...Caroline? Why won't you look?

CAROLINE

I am in a hurry to finish this letter.

EMMA

Rebecca? Stop moving the furniture around and look at that wall. Why won't you look? Both of you...Oh! Look! That awful shadow! What is it? Caroline, Rebecca...look!

REBECCA

Oh, Caroline, there it is again, there it is again!

EMMA

Caroline Glynn, you look! Look! What is that dreadful shadow?

CAROLINE

How should I know?

REBECCA

It has been there every night since he died!

EMMA

Every night?

CAROLINE

Yes! He died Thursday and this is Saturday... that makes three nights.

EMMA

It...it looks like...like...

CAROLINE

I know what it looks like well enough. I've got eyes in my head.

REBECCA

It looks like Edward...Only...

EMMA

Yes, it does...only...Oh, it is awful! What is it, Caroline?

CAROLINE

I ask you again, how should I know? I see it there like you. How should I know any more than you?

EMMA

Where does it come from? It *must* be something in the room.

REBECCA

We moved everything in the room the first night it came. It is not anything in the room.

CAROLINE

Of course it is something in the room! How you act! What do you mean talking like this? Of course it is something in the room.

EMMA

Of course it is...it must be something in the room.

REBECCA

It is not anything in the room.

(KNOCK. DOOR OPENS)

HENRY

It's just me again. What are you ladies talking about? Why are you all standing there? Oh my God, what is that?

EMMA

It must be due to something in the room.

HENRY

But...but....what is it? A stain?

REBECCA

A...shadow.

HENRY

A shadow? What? I mean...

CAROLINE

What are you gawking at, Henry?

HENRY

Must be the way the light hits a piece of furniture....

REBECCA

We tried moving all the furniture.
(FURNITURE MOVING ABOUT)

HENRY

It's got to be! What other explanation can there be? What?
Why are you all staring at me? This is ludicrous.
Absolutely...here, this chair! No...not the chair...this plant?
No! This sculpture? No! Damn it!

(CRASH)

Well now (Laughs)...isn't this an absurdity? Such a to-do
about a shadow.

EMMA

Yes...

CAROLINE

I think you have broken the chair that Edward was fond of...

HENRY

Stop seething over a chair, Caroline. You look like you're
ready to bare your fangs. There now, alright? It's just as good
as ever. Ha! Did I scare you, dear sisters? I should think you
might be used to me by this time. You know my way of wanting
to leap to the bottom of a mystery, and that shadow does
look...very strange...and I thought if there was any way of
accounting for it I would like to without any delay.

CAROLINE

You don't seem to have succeeded.

HENRY
Well, there is no accounting for shadows...A man is a fool to try to account for shadows.

(DINNER BELL)

There now, time for dinner. Come, sisters...let me lead the way to the dining room.

REBECCA
(Whispers) Caroline, I can't sit in that room this evening. My knees are trembling.

CAROLINE
Very well, Rebecca. Everyone, we will sit in the south room. It isn't as damp as the study, and I have a cold.

(MUSIC, CLOCK STRIKES)

REBECCA
(Whispers) Emma, where are you going? It's ten o'clock.

EMMA
(Whispers) I saw Henry go in that room before...I want to see what he's doing. The door is open.

REBECCA
It can't close...it's swollen from the dampness.

EMMA
Shush...let's peek. What is Caroline doing?

REBECCA
She is in the parlor, sewing. What's Henry doing in there? Can you see?

EMMA
He's examining the shadow on the wall again. Carrying the lamp about the room. He's got a sword...he's striking out at the air...as if there might be something invisible in the room. It's not working.

REBECCA
Now, what is he doing?

EMMA

He's just standing there. Clenching his fists. Frustrated. Let's go find Caroline.

(MUSIC)

You should have seen him, Caroline. He looked like a demon. Have you got any of that old wine in the house? I don't feel as if I could stand much more mystery and suspense...

CAROLINE

Yes, there's plenty, you can have some when you go to bed.

EMMA

I think we had all better take some. You should have seen him. Like a man possessed. Pacing up and down like that. Staring at the shadow. He was livid. His blue eyes, they looked like bottomless pits.

REBECCA

Bottomless pits.

CAROLINE

Is he still in there?

EMMA

I think so. And, it's nearly midnight.

CAROLINE

Well, we should be off to bed. We have a funeral to conduct tomorrow.

(MUSIC)

REBECCA

(Sobs) I don't know if I'll ever stop crying. I miss Edward terribly.

CAROLINE

Well, the funeral went well enough. I'm glad it was just us...I don't care to see anyone else at this time. No relatives, no friends and no strangers. Where's Henry?

EMMA

He's gone back into that room again carrying a lamp. Seems he's determined to get to the bottom of that mysterious shadow. Shush, here he comes.

HENRY

Sisters...I have something to tell you...

CAROLINE

Yes?

HENRY

I am leaving tomorrow...I have to go to the city for three days or so.

CAROLINE

But...you never go anywhere, Henry.

EMMA

And, what about your practice? How can you leave your patients? You've been neglecting them, you know, ever since Edward's death.

HENRY

I know, but, there is no other way. I have had a telegram from Dr. Mitford.

EMMA

Consultation?

HENRY

I have business. Well, I think I'll go upstairs to my room awhile...and pack. I'm taking the 6:15 in the morning.

EMMA

Well...that's strange.

REBECCA

Everything is very strange.

CAROLINE

What do you mean?

REBECCA

Nothing.

(MUSIC)

EMMA

We've not heard a word from Henry and it's been three days. Something is definitely wrong. The idea of a doctor leaving his patients at such a time as this, and the idea of a consultation lasting three days! There is no sense in it, and no word from him? I don't understand it.

REBECCA

I don't either. Emma? Where are you going? Emma...?

EMMA

Shush!

REBECCA

Is something wrong, Emma? Emma...why are you going into that room again? Don't go in there. It's so dark. You don't have a lamp. Caroline! Caroline! Come...something is wrong. Emma...she just stood up and went out into the hall and walked into the room. She won't answer me. I'm too scared to follow her. Come and see....

CAROLINE

Emma? Are you in here?

(DOOR BELL)

Rebecca, see who it is...go now! Caroline? It's me, Caroline...what are you doing in here, sister? Here... here's the lamp, dear. Stop staring at the wall...stop...Oh dear Lord in Heaven!

EMMA

See? See the wall! There are two shadows now...

CAROLINE

Two shadows! Two!

REBECCA

(Screams) Aaaahhh!

CAROLINE

Rebecca! What's wrong? What's that in your hand, dear?
What are you holding...?

REBECCA

It's a telegram...it says...Henry...

CAROLINE

What about Henry?

REBECCA

He's dead!

_____

THE THING IN THE UPPER ROOM
By Dan Bianchi
From A Story By Arthur Morrison

Cast - 3m
Running Time - 14 min
Synopsis - A boarder's room is possessed by a murdering spirit

(MUSIC)

NARRATOR
"They say the upstairs room is haunted. Who says? Idiots, that's who. Superstitious fools. Can you believe that the previous landlord had not even rented the space for years? A perfectly good apartment here in the city. Well, it's rented now. To me. And, at a great price. It doesn't matter that it's old. I prefer that to a modern high rise, cold and unfeeling. This place...this place has character. Yes. I suppose that's what you might call it. It was built before the Civil War. A boarding house. God knows what had gone on here over the years. People of all sorts, coming and going. I wonder what had happened here, in these rooms, to have made the previous landlord so afraid to rent it? A murder, perhaps? A suicide? Visions of the victim wandering the hall at midnight?"

LANDLORD
You heard what happened to the last man who last lived here in this apartment...what, ten years ago?

NARRATOR
What's that?

LANDLORD
Shot himself to death.

NARRATOR
Really?

LANDLORD
Yeah, the police were knocking down the door at the time. They come to arrest him for murder.

NARRATOR

"Well, that solves that question. But, I get no further details. This landlord doesn't seem to be a believer in the supernatural. He's here for the rent."

LANDLORD

Here, let me open a window and get some air in here. The chimney still works, so if you're here by winter, you can use the fireplace for heat. I don't know why people think the room is haunted. Look at it. It's just a plain old empty room. With a plain old chair and a bed and a table. In the middle of the city. It's not as if it's out in the woods all alone on a moonlit night, you know? The light's good. You got morning light. What are you, a writer?

NARRATOR

We shall see.

LANDLORD

But, you can afford the rent, right?

NARRATOR

Oh yes, it's fine.

LANDLORD

I mean...if you should hear anything...any gossip from the neighbors...silly innuendoes about the place...

NARRATOR

Oh, I won't take it seriously.

LANDLORD

No...of course not. Hey, you're a writer...maybe, you'll be inspired to write a fright story in a magazine. Only don't mention the address. Well, here's the key. Just knock on my door downstairs if you need anything.

(DOOR CLOSE)

NARRATOR

"My own key! My own room. I can't wait to tell my friends that I've rented a real haunted studio. I've never considered writing fright stories before, but, I may just take him up on it. It is a cheap, tawdry little place from another time, isn't it? You'd think he might have put a lick of paint to it by now. But...it looked to me as if he couldn't wait to get out of here just now...he may not have been in here for years.

(WINDOW SLAMS SHUT)

What the...! "The window...slammed shut all by itself. Well, right on cue. Must have been a spirit from beyond! Ha! Ugh...what's that stench? Ugh...it's murderous, takes my breath away. May be a dead rat in the walls. No, it's not a settled odor...it's something that's passing by me. Gone now. May be chimney fumes from outside or...well, I might as well get unpacked. I don't...I mean...I don't know why I keep looking over my shoulder. You see? The power of suggestion. How it can command your mind to...fool! What I need is a good smoke. Where's my pipe? Ah! I'll just lie down on the bed and light up. Relax. Take it all in. Here now...what's that? On the windowsill...didn't see it before. Well, will you look at that? That is a dagger...something Oriental...a Malay dagger I think. I wonder how it got here? Left behind from the previous tenant? Murderous looking thing...but, a beautifully carved handle...a bird's head with a curved beak and an eye, a red gem...that can't be a ruby? A twisted body turning into a snake. Fascinating. What's it doing here? Mesmerizing. Well, I'll put it down here on the table and give it to the landlord later on. I'll just...hey! How did that chair....how did it get over here? It was just over there against the wall.

(CHURCH BELLS)

"Is someone playing tricks here? No, I see...I must have moved it while I was so captivated by that knife...didn't realize what I was doing. I suppose. Brrrrr...it's cold in here. But, the window's closed. Six o'clock? Is it six already? I can't stand around here talking to myself. I have to meet my friends. Still I...I...I can't help feeling...I'm being watched. I don't mean from outside the room, as if through a keyhole. No...it's as if someone is in here with me. Someone...or something. What! Damn! It's just you...your own reflection in that old mirror, idiot. Ha! Thought someone was staring at me. Like in that old Japanese story...the demon-possessed man...every time he looked in the mirror...he saw not himself, but, the demon. Ugh...there's that stink again. Turning my stomach. Making me nauseous. Put that damned blade in your suitcase. Lock it up. Oh, I have to sit down. Making my mind swim. You're being ridiculous, you know? Remember that story you had read? About the haunted house wherein it was shown that the house actually *was* haunted…by the spirit of *fear*, and nothing else. That's what is happening here. There's nothing supernatural, you fool. See how easy it is to be persuaded? You let your imagination run wild and the next thing you know…(Yawns) Well, suddenly…I'm very tired. Very tired. I don't think I'll go anywhere tonight. I should stay in, get some rest, get used to my new place. Getting dark. Where's the candle? Ah, here we go…let me get a match.

(STRIKES MATCH)

"There now. Very cozy, isn't it. The landlord, at least, provided me with clean blankets and a pillow. Very nice. I should do some writing. But…(Yawns) Oh, my…I am tired…I'm so…" (Snores)

(MUSIC)

LANDLORD

Good morning!

NARRATOR

Good morning.

LANDLORD

Sleep well?

NARRATOR

Well, now that you mention it…not really. I mean, I did sleep like a log. But, such dreams. Horrible dreams.

LANDLORD

What about?

NARRATOR

Nothing, nothing. I can't even remember them. You wouldn't have an aspirin, would you?

LANDLORD

Headache?

NARRATOR

Yeah.

LANDLORD

Hangover?

NARRATOR

No. I haven't touched a drop all night. "I wonder if I should tell him about the dagger with the ruby eye? When I awoke before...there it was on the table, staring at me. Didn't I lock it in my suitcase last night?

LANDLORD

Here's your aspirin.

NARRATOR

Thanks.

LANDLORD

Hey...uhm...you haven't...seen anything strange...?

NARRATOR

What? You mean, the ghost? No, no ghost.

LANDLORD

No! Of course not.

NARRATOR

Well, I'm just going out now. To meet some friends at a café around the block.

LANDLORD

Have a nice day!

(MUSIC, TRAFFIC)

NARRATOR

John!

JOHN

Hello!

NARRATOR

Sit down! Have a coffee with me.

JOHN

I thought you'd be hard at work on your novel by now. And here I find you just sitting around, lounging like the bourgeoisie. Hey, did you hear about the murder last night? It's all over the Journal.

NARRATOR

What? No. I haven't read the papers.

JOHN

Sure. And we know the victim.

NARRATOR

What?

JOHN

Well, we don't *know* him…but, you remember the old man who sits on the stoop over by McSorley's Tavern? He's always there, day or night.

NARRATOR

Murdered?

JOHN

Yep. Poor old guy. Stabbed to death. It says, stabbed at least, twenty times. Who would want to do that to the old guy? It wasn't for money, that's for sure. He hadn't a dime. I doubt if he had any enemies. Says he was viciously attacked just before dawn. Probably by a homicidal maniac. No clues as to who did it. Hey, you alright? You look pale as a…

NARRATOR

Oh, I…haven't been sleeping very well…bad dreams and all that.

JOHN

And here I am talking about a gruesome murder. Let's forget about the coffee. What you need is a good bottle of Burgundy. And a good steak.

(MUSIC)

NARRATOR

"Well, that was just what I needed. A good meal. Good drink. Calm my nerves. Make me forget about...all that other stuff. I mean, I hate when people who believe in all that mumbo jumbo...they're so stupid. Ha! And to think ...Me? Of all people. I mean, I *am* a college graduate, after all.

(CHURCH BELLS)

"After midnight. Time for bed. And tomorrow...I shall write one...two chapters of my novel. I promise. Time to put the candle out...'Out, out, brief candle! Life's but a walking shadow, a poor player that struts and frets his hour upon the stage ...and then is heard no more... it is a tale told by an idiot (Yawns) full of sound and fury,
Signifying nothing...'

(MUSIC, SNORES)

"Ahhhh! What? What! Damn! Can't catch my breath ...where am I? What's going on? It's dark. I'm not in my bed...I'm on the floor! Oh God...oh God...I must have fallen...

(POLICE BELL RINGS IN
STREET. CROWD. CRIES)

"What's going on? In the street?"

VOICE (DISTANT)

Murder! Murder!

NARRATOR

"What's all this? Get up, you fool. Go to the window. See what it's all about. My legs...trembling. I'm covered in sweat. The window! Open it! Hold on... what...I'm still dressed? I'm not in my bed clothes. I'm even... wearing ...my hat?

(OUTSIDE NOISE GROWS FAINT)

"They're going away now. Why am I fully dressed? I'm sure when I had come home...I got myself ready for bed and...where are the damned matches? I left them on the table right here...Aha...

(STRIKES MATCH)

Ahhhhhh! What was that? Something wet…something sticky… something….there it is! The knife…lying there on the table. But it was just in my hand. You mean, I held it all that time and didn't realize…? My hands….they're wet…smeared, dripping…with…blood. This can't be…I must be dreaming… another nightmare…another…ahhhh! Look! In the mirror…in the mirror…staring back at me….look, that's not you…those glowing red eyes …glistening like rubies…that's not me…then, who…what is it? It's…it's…not me…whatever it is…it's not me! But, there it is. It's here, in this room, right now and… The match! It's gone out! It's dark…it's dark…oh Jesus…"

THE DEMON LOVER
By Dan Bianchi
From A Story By Elizabeth Bowen

Cast - 1m, 1w
Running Time - 14 min
Synopsis - A woman's dead lover returns to haunt her

(CLOCK CHIMES)

CATHERINE

"Is it the end of the day already? Where does the time go?
Why am I here? Yes, why, Catherine? Well, I was in the city
today, so I thought I'd drop by the house to get a few
things...bring them out to the summer house. Oh, it's so hot
and stuffy in here.

(THUNDER)

"A hot, steamy, rainy day. Why not open the big window in the
hall, let some air in here?

(WINDOW OPEN)

"Alone now...so quiet...yet, now, I notice things. For instance,
that yellow smoke stain upon the white marble mantelpiece...
there's a ring left by a vase on the top of the writing desk...the
bruise in the wallpaper where the doorknob always hits the
wall. At least, it's not dusty in here. But, it does have the
aroma of a cold chimney. Now, what do I want? Oh yes...
upstairs...in the bedroom. Well, what's this? Someone left a
letter on the hall table...a letter addressed to *me*? Perhaps,
Mrs.Brown left it there. But, even she's been away on vacation.
Who would put a letter on the table? And why did the post
office even deliver it? They know the house is empty for the
summer. It's not an advertisement. It's not a bill. It's
addressed to *me*. No one even knows I'm here today or if I'd
return for months. I didn't plan to come here, at all. Why didn't
someone send it on to me? This is annoying. It doesn't even
have a stamp. It can't be important.

(RIPS OPEN LETTER)

MAN'S VOICE

"Dear Catherine... You will not have forgotten that today is our anniversary. The years have gone by so quickly. In view of the fact that nothing has changed, I shall rely upon you to keep your promise. I was sorry to see you leave the city, but, was satisfied that you would be back in time. You may expect me, therefore, at the hour arranged today. Until then . . . M."

CATHERINE

"Today? Today? How can that be? And what is this all about...'I shall rely upon you to keep your promise?' Someone is coming here? Today? To meet me? That's what it says. Today. Oh God...no...no...

(THUNDER, CLOCK TICKS, STRIKES)

"'The hour arranged?'" My God, *what* hour? How should I...? After twenty five years? Today! Twenty five years ago...I remember now...the soldier in the garden. On leave. But, I was only a young girl then. Standing there in the shadows. Saying good bye to him under a tree. I put out my hand and...touched the brass buttons on his uniform and..."

MAN'S VOICE

Are you cold, Catherine?

CATHERINE

You're going away, so far away.

MAN'S VOICE

Not so far as you think.

CATHERINE

I don't understand.

MAN'S VOICE

You don't have to. You will. You know what we said...what we promised each other.

CATHERINE

But, that was...suppose you...I mean, suppose?

MAN'S VOICE

I shall be with you...sooner or later. You won't forget that. You need do nothing but wait.

CATHERINE

"He didn't even kiss me. In an instant, he was gone. I remember becoming overwhelmed with emotion...right out there in the garden...I ran back into the house...to my mother. 'Mother! What shall I do? He's gone!'"

MAN'S VOICE

(ECHO) I shall be with you...sooner or later. You won't forget that. You need do nothing but wait.

(MUSIC)

CATHERINE

"Two months later...the letter came...from the Army. Missing. Presumed killed. My family consoled me, best they could, even though they had never known him. They had hoped I'd get over it...give it a year or so. They didn't expect that grief worked differently on me...Yes, I totally shut out the past. For years, I didn't care about any men. But, by the time I was thirty...yes, I found William Drover. And, I married him. That was a relief for everyone. Settled down. The children were born. Get up off your knees, Catherine. Get up now. This letter, either from the dead or living, is a threat. A threat to your family. In a moment, all you know of your happy life can be over. The letter writer is letting you know that. In your own house. In *my* house.

(THUNDER)

"Shut the window! Quickly!

(WINDOW CLOSE)

"Maybe, if I shut my eyes, you know... And when I open them the letter will be...Still there. On the bed. Don't even think of ...no, that's too weird. There's nothing supernatural about this. But, no one knew I'd stop at the house today. I didn't know myself until I drove by to take a look and...Well, someone knew, Catherine. Obviously, they left this letter here addressed to you. Someone put it here on the hall table. A living person. Mrs.Brown. It had to be her. But, still...she wouldn't have left it here for me. She'd have dropped it in the mail to our summer home. There's no sign that anyone else has been here. But, if that's so, then...? *No*, letters don't just appear on hall tables. But, it has *my* name on it and what's more it has today's date. There must be some human...living ...person who is behind this. Still...only Mrs.Brown and I have keys. I suppose burglars can find a way no matter what...but, nothing has been taken. On the other hand...it *is* possible...you may not be alone in this house at this very minute. Here you are, by yourself, upstairs...and someone might be waiting for you down there. Waiting. Until when...'the hour arranged?' Perhaps, you'd better lock the bedroom door.

(DOOR LOCK)

"Why lock yourself in? Maybe, you should run straight down the stairs, don't stop, right out the front door. You still have to catch a train, you know? You have a family, little boys, waiting for you back at the summer house. Well, I'm not going until I collect the things I was going to take back with me in the first place. Shoes...the black formals I'll need for the community ball next week...and Tommy needs more underwear... and...It's no good. I can't keep my mind on this. How can I carry, much less run with all this and the shopping bags I've left downstairs...a taxi? That's right...a taxi! Just ring them up and they'll be here in no time and you'll walk calmly downstairs..."

(DIALS PHONE)

Hello? Hello...information? Hello...?

(TAPPING RECEIVER)

"No signal. Cut off...no phone. Alright, now, this is too much. You're in danger now, you realize that? The phone is dead? And, someone is probably downstairs ...Oh yeah, I'd say I'm in *big* danger. In fact, he may even be right outside that door. I don't know why. Think! *Why* are you here? Why now? It's not as if he was ever kind to me, not really. I don't remember that he was kind to me. Mother said he never considered my feelings, at all. Not really. Sure, he wanted me. *Sex.* That was all it was. That was what I meant to him. Not *love.* Not love, not knowing a person *well.* Wanting all the best for that person. What did *he* do, to make me promise like that? I can't remember….well, yes, you can remember, Catherine. Actually, it's all very clear. Twenty-five years ago, today. I remember …not only all that I said and did… but. the complete suspension of *my* existence during that August week. I was not myself…they all told me so at the time. My family, my friends. I didn't listen to them. I remember all that…yes, but, there is one thing I cannot remember as hard as I try. I just cannot remember his face. So, wherever he may be waiting, I won't know him.

(CLOCK CHIMES)

"Wasting time here worrying about a face I can't remember. The thing is to get to the taxi before it gets any later. Just slip down to the street and down to the corner drug store and call for a taxi. The taxi driver will take me back here, I'll bring him into the house to help me with my bags and all will be fine. Sure, that's the plan. A taxi driver. All you need to do, Catherine, is to unlock your door…

(UNLOCK DOOR, DOOR CREAKS OPEN)

"That's it. Listen?

(THUNDER)

"Now get to the staircase. Nothing.

(WIND)

"Whoa! What's that? A draft…I think a door or window downstairs just opened…whoever's down there must have left. I'm down the stairs now…heading for the front door. You're gonna make it, girl.

(DOOR OPENS)

"Well, the rain has stopped…just a few more steps and you'll be on the sidewalk. Look at the street…kind of quiet. As if everyone is gone for the summer.

(HIGH HEEL FOOTSTEPS)

"Listen to yourself walking, strutting at high speed toward the corner drug store.

(STREET NOISE)

"There you are now, Catherine. Buses and people and cars coming and going. A woman with a baby carriage …a few people on bicycles… a workman and a wheel barrow. The ordinary flow of life. And, parked out front of the drug store…just what you're looking for…a taxi. Ready and waiting for you." Taxi!

> (OPENS CAR DOOR, CLOSES.
> CHURCH BELL STRIKES SEVEN.
> CAR TAKES OFF)

Driver! Can you hear me from back here? I didn't tell you where I have to go.

> (KNOCKS ON GLASS)

Driver! You didn't ask me where I'm going…how can you just drive off like this and…you're driving like a madman, please stop!

> (CAR SKIDS TO HALT. GLASS PARTITION
> SLIDES OPEN)

Now, I'm going to report you, mister…you just wait and…

MAN'S VOICE

Hello, Catherine…

CATHERINE

My God! It's…you!

MAN'S VOICE

I'm so glad you've waited for me…

> (SHE SCREAMS, CAR TAKES
> OFF, SHE BANGS ON DOORS)

CATHERINE

Stop! Stop! I won't go with you! I've got a family! I won't….

> (CAR RACES AWAY)

THE KISS
By Dan Bianchi

Cast - 3m, 1w
Running Time - 14 min
Synopsis - Two lovers call an end to a relationship

(CITY STREETS, TRAFFIC, MUSIC)

NARRATOR
At night, in a nearly deserted office building, there are the
occasional faint sounds of the cleaners at work...down the hall
somewhere...

(VOICES, VACUUM
CLEANER, DOOR SLAM)

he still sits at his desk, after all of his fellow co-workers have
left, but, he's not alone...he's sitting sideways now, regarding
the other occupant of the room. She's not beautiful...no need
to be. And, he doesn't regard her as a sexual object. Or, so, he
thinks. Certainly, he loves when she walks close to him...and
the fragrance of her corn-gold hair and the sight of her
voluptuous figure...and she knows it. Until now, there has
been no physical contact between them. Tonight, she knows,
the barriers will be down... tonight, they will kiss.

MAN
The Lord made the world and then He made this rotten old
office. Into it He put you...and me. Whatever it's taken to make
you, *you*...and me...is not the point. It is enough that we have
realized, heart and soul, and body, that you are mine and I am
yours.

WOMAN
Yes.

NARRATOR
He falls silent again, his eyes feast on her hungrily. She feels
them and longs for his touch. But, there is only his voice.

MAN
I want you. The first moment I saw you I wanted you. I thought,

then, that, whatever the cost, I will have you. That was in the early days of our talks here...before you made it so courageously clear to me that it would never be possible for you to ignore my marriage and come to me. That *is* still true, isn't it?

NARRATOR

She moves slightly, like a dreamer in pain, as. again, she faces the situation she has hated through many a sleepless night.

WOMAN

Yes. And because of that, you are going away tomorrow.

MAN

Yes. I have to.

NARRATOR

They look at each other across the foot or two of intervening space. It is a mournful look. But, even beneath their suffering, her eyes voice the tremulous waiting of her lips.

MAN

You are the most wonderful woman in the world...the bravest, the most completely understanding. The most charitable. I suppose I ought to thank you for it all. I can't...that's not my way. I have always demanded of you, demanded enormously, and received more than I deserve. Now I am going to ask this last thing of you... will you, out of the goodness in your heart...go away? Upstairs, anywhere...and come back in ten minutes' time? By then, I shall have cleared out.

NARRATOR

She looks at him, almost incredulously, lips parted. Suddenly, she seems to be a child.

WOMAN

You...! But, you *must* kiss me before you go. You *must*! You...simply *must*."

NARRATOR

For the space of a flaming moment it seems that in one stride he would cross to her side, catch her and hold her.

MAN

For God's sake!

NARRATOR

He turns away to stamp down his emotions. Then, with some effort, he regains his self-control.

MAN

Listen, I want to kiss you so much that I dare not even get to my feet. Do you understand what that means? Think of it, just for a moment, and then realize that, I am *not* going to kiss you. And, I have kissed many women in my time, too, and shall kiss more, no doubt.

WOMAN

But, it's not because of that...?

MAN

That I'm holding back? No. Neither is it because I deny the torture of kissing you once and letting you go. It's because I'm afraid...for *you*.

WOMAN

For *me*?

MAN

Listen. You have unfolded your beliefs to me, laid them all out. Though I don't believe in them, I realize that I must honor those beliefs. It makes me revere you, more than you can ever believe. I have put you in a shrine and knelt to you... every time you have sat in that chair and talked with me, I have worshipped you.

WOMAN

It would not change things...if you kissed me.

MAN

I don't believe that. Neither do you...no, you don't! In your heart of hearts you admit that a woman like you is not kissed for the first and last time by a man like me. Suppose I kissed you now? I should awaken something in you that, up to now, has been half asleep. You're young and pulsing with life, and there are...thank Heaven!...few layers of that damnable young-girl shyness over you. The world would call you *naive*, I suppose.

WOMAN
But, I don't..

MAN
Oh, Lord, you must see it's all or nothing! You surely understand that after I leave you... you won't go against your morality, perhaps, but, you will adjust it, in spite of yourself, to meet your desires! I cannot...safely...kiss you.

WOMAN
But, you are going away for good!

MAN
For good! What? Do you think that ends things? If you want me so much you'll come to think it is right and good to want me. Wouldn't you find me, send for me, call for me? And I should come. God! I can see the look in your eyes now... when the want has been satisfied, you won't need your beliefs anymore. I'm right, aren't I?

NARRATOR
She nods. Speech is too difficult. With the movement a strand of the corn-gold hair comes tumbling down the side of her face.

MAN
Then, that being the case, I shall not attempt so much as to touch your hand before you leave the room.

WOMAN
Tell me once again, You do *want* to kiss me?

MAN
Alright! I do want to kiss you! I want to kiss you. If there is any way of cutting off tomorrow...all the tomorrows ...with the danger they hold for us...I would kiss you. I would kiss you, and kiss you, and kiss you!

(MUSIC)

NARRATOR

Where her feet takes her during the thousand, thousand years it takes for him to leave…she can't say, but, she finds herself at last at the top of the great building, at an open window, leaning out, with the rain beating into her eyes. Far below her, the lights twinkle and the sounds of the city waft up to her window. But, her ears hold only the memory of a man's footsteps… the eager footsteps that never lingered a second on their way to her…that sound will never come again. The raindrops lay like tears upon her face. She brushes them aside, and, rising, puts up her hands to feel the rain lying heavy on her hair. The coldness of her limbs surprise her faintly. He should be gone by now. Downstairs, she goes again, back to the office, the echoes mocking every step. She closes the door of the room behind her and idly clears a scrap of paper from a chair. Mechanically, her hands go to the litter on his desk. She straightens it all before she realizes that there is no longer any need. Tomorrow will bring a voice she does not know. A stranger will enter into her room. There will be a new tone of voice. A barrier of formality. From now on, it will only be work, and food, and sleep. For her, these things will make life…life that has been love.

She puts on her hat and coat. The room seems smaller somehow and shabbier. The shaded lights, once inviting, now merely irritating. The whimsical disorder of books and papers now reveal only an uncompleted task. Gone is the glamour and the promise and the good comradeship. He has taken them all. She faces tomorrow, and tomorrow, and tomorrow empty-handed…in her heart the memory of words that have seared and healed in a breath, and the dead dream of a kiss. Her throat aches with the pain of it. And, then, suddenly…

(DOOR DISTANT SLAMS)

Is he coming back? It's him, isn't it? She stiffens. For one instant, mind and body, are rigid with the sheer wonder of it. Then, as the atmosphere of the room surges back, tense with vitality, her mind leaps forward to welcome him. He's coming back, coming back! The words hammer themselves out to the rhythm of the eager footsteps that never linger so much as a second on their way to her…

(FOOTSTEPS IN HALLWAY,

DOOR OPENS)

MAN
I've come back. I've come back to kiss you. Dear...*dear*!

NARRATOR
She throws up her hand to check him in his stride towards her. Words stammer to her lips.

WOMAN
Why...but,...this isn't...I don't understand! All you said...it was true, surely? It was cruel of you to make me know it was true and then come back!

MAN
Let me kiss you...let me, let me! I must kiss you, I must kiss you.

WOMAN
No, no, you can't...you can't play with me! You said you were afraid for me, and you made me afraid, too...of my weakness...of the danger...of my longing for you...

MAN
Let me kiss you! Just let me, just let me.

NARRATOR
His arms hold her, his face touches hers.

WOMAN
Aren't you afraid anymore? Has a miracle happened ...may we kiss in spite of tomorrow?

NARRATOR
Inch by inch she relaxes. All thought slips away into a great white light that holds no tomorrows, nor any fear of them, nor of herself, nor of anything. The light creeps to her feet, rises to her heart, her head. Through the radiance come his words.

MAN
Yes, a miracle. Oh, my dear...my darling girl. Don't you see? I've come back to kiss you...

WOMAN

Kiss me, then…

(MUSIC)

NARRATOR

In a daze now. But, she's aware that he's released her. She raises her head, then rests it against the rough tweed of his shoulder, leaving it there, her shock of long, corn-gold hair. She laughs shakily and then attempts to remove a strand…but, he catches her fingers and holds them to his face. And, with that movement and his look there comes over her in a wave the shame of her surrender… a shame that has damaged her pride. She turns blindly away.

WOMAN

Please, let me go now. I want to be alone. I want to…please don't talk to me anymore tonight. Tomorrow…

NARRATOR

She's at the door, groping for the handle. Behind her, she hears his voice, speaking tenderly…

MAN

I shall always kneel to you…in your shrine.

(DOOR CLOSES. MUSIC)

NARRATOR

Now, she's moving down the hall. She's left him in the room behind her. He'll wait there long enough to allow her to leave the building. Almost immediately, it seems, she's downstairs in the hall, reaching the entrance where she is met by a group of white-faced, silent men. The night watchman, Charlie, shakes his head as she approaches.

(POLICE SIREN APPROACHES, CROWD NOISE)

WOMAN

What's going on? Is anything the matter? What's happened? Charlie?

CHARLIE

Yes, Miss Carryll. You can't go out this way tonight. You'd best be going out the door down the other end.

WOMAN

Why is there a police car outside? Did something happen?

NARRATOR

Some powerful premonition is stirring in her...she cannot simply leave it be.

WOMAN

Has there been an accident? Who's that lying on the sidewalk?

NARRATOR

Then, almost under her feet, she sees a dark pool washing over the pavement. Blood.

WOMAN

Oh my God!

CHARLIE

Officer...this young lady is his secretary. She must be the last who seen him alive.   Probably, half an hour ago, I'd say. He come down here and says, Miss Carryll's still working upstairs...don't lock her in.   Then, he just steps outside and this car comes barreling down the street and...pow! I called the ambulance but...

(SHE SCREAMS)

NARRATOR

Her cry cuts into his words as she flings herself forward. Past Charlie, past the burly policemen. They attempt to detain her, but, they can't stop her. Unhearing, unheeding, she forces her way into the glare of headlights and twirling red police lights...and there, on the sidewalk, in the pool of blood, covered by a sheet, it lies.

WOMAN

It can't be...it can't be...

NARRATOR

Before she even reaches the corpse, knowledge has dropped upon her like a cloak.   Her face turns grey as she pulls back the sheet... the victim is a gory mess, unrecognizable...but, she breathes a momentary sigh of relief...

WOMAN
There! You see? It can't be him...it can't...it...

NARRATOR
Against the rough tweed of his shoulder lays a long strand of corn-gold hair.

SMEE
By Dan Bianchi
From A Story By A.M.Burrage

Cast – 3m,2w
Running Time – 14 min
Synopsis - A man encounters a ghostly woman

(MUSIC, PARTY SOUNDS)

JACKSON

"Five years ago my cousin Harry and his wife Violet invited me, along with a lot of other guests, to spend Christmas with them. They own an old house out in Miller Place, with so many passages and staircases, you can get lost in them. Unfortunately, I couldn't get away from my job on Madison Avenue until late on Christmas Eve. So, I am the last to arrive, just in time for dinner. Harry's wife Violet introduces me to everyone and we all sit down at the table…which is, perhaps, why I don't hear the name of a tall, dark haired, beauty whom I haven't met before. Everyone is in rather a hurry and I am always bad at catching people's names. She looks cold and clever. She doesn't look at all friendly, but, she looks interesting, and I wonder whom she is. But…I don't ask, because I'm sure that someone will speak to her by name during the meal. Now, there are twelve of us, including our hosts. We are all young or trying to be young. Harry and Violet are the oldest, and their seventeen-year old son Reggie is the youngest. He's the one who suggests we play the game of Smee when the talk turns to games."

BOB
What does Smee mean anyway?

HARRY
It's a bastardization of "It's me!" Smee?

BOB
Ah! Smee!

PEGGY
Smee!

HARRY
Now...just one thing...If we are going to play games in the dark, please be careful of the back stairs on the first floor. A door leads to them, and I've often thought about taking the door off. In the dark a stranger to the house could think they were walking into a room. A girl really did break her neck on those stairs.

JACKSON
How did that happen?

HARRY
It was about ten years ago, before we came here. There was a party and they were playing hide and seek. This girl was looking for somewhere to hide. She heard somebody coming, and ran along the hall to get away. She opened the door, thinking it led to a bedroom. I guess she planned to hide in there until the seeker had gone. Unfortunately, it was the door that led to the back stairs. She fell straight down to the bottom of the stairs. She was dead when they picked her up. So, please, all of you, please be careful.

PEGGY
Well, that's a depressing story.

BOB
Still, it's not like any of us knew the poor girl...and we don't want to feel sad on Christmas Eve, now, do we?

VIOLET
Let's play *Smee!*

HARRY
Reggie, make sure all of the lights are turned off in the house.

VIOLET
At least in here, we have the light from the fire place. Harry, you hand out the paper.

HARRY
Now, if you don't know how to play *Smee.*

JACKSON

And, I don't!

PEGGY

Me neither.

HARRY

I've got twelve sheets of paper, folks. Eleven of them are blank, and one of them has *Smee* written on it. I'll mix them all up, then we'll each take one. The person who gets the paper with *Smee* on it has to hide. Then, I'll blow the whistle and the rest of us go to look for *Smee* in the dark. *Smee* can hide wherever he, or she, likes. If you run into someone...you ask him if he's *Smee.* If he's not, you just move on. But, if he is, he's not allowed to reply. So, then, you are captured and you stay with *Smee* until all the rest of us eventually find you and we're all captured. Most importantly, there is no talking when you are captured. Got that?

PEGGY

I think so.

BOB

Sure!

JACKSON

I get it.

HARRY

Ok, let's start picking...

JACKSON

"Well, luckily, I draw a blank. A moment later, all the electric lights go out. And then...

(WHISTLE)

"We all rush to the door. For five or ten minutes we find our way up and down passages and in and out of rooms, all in near total darkness. I can hear others challenging others..."

VIOLET

(Distant) *Smee?*

BOB

(Distant) *Smee!*

JACKSON

Eventually, the noise dies down, and I'm guessing that someone has found *Smee.* After a time I find a group of people all sitting on some narrow stairs. I challenge, but, receive no answer. That means *Smee* is amongst them. I join the group. Two more players arrive. Each one hurries to avoid being last. Bob is last.

PEGGY

You're the loser, Bob!

BOB

Thank you very much.

HARRY

Wait. I think we're all here now, aren't we? Let me light a match.

(STRIKES MATCH)

Let's see...one, two...four, six...eight...ten...twelve, thirteen. No wait...how can that be. There's one too many. Ow! Damn match burned my finger...Hold on...

(STRIKES MATCH)

Two, four...eight, ten, twelve...thirteen? That can't be! There are thirteen people here!

JACKSON

Harry! Are you sure you haven't counted yourself twice?

HARRY

Reggie! Bring a flash light from the drawer in the hall!

PEGGY

What's the matter, Harry? Did you forget how to count?

HARRY

That's it...shine it over here. Let's begin again, shall we? Two, four, six, eight, twelve! Now there are twelve!

BOB

Oh...*now* there are twelve!

PEGGY

Now there are twelve?

HARRY

Well, I was sure I counted thirteen twice.

VIOLET

You may be right, Harry.

BOB

What?

VIOLET

I thought there was somebody sitting two steps above me.
Have you moved, Peg?

PEGGY

Not me.

VIOLET

But, I thought there was somebody sitting between Peg and
me.

BOB

Oooh...now *that's* mysterious.

JACKSON

"Just for a moment there is an uncomfortable something in the
air. A cold finger seems to touch us all. For that moment we all
feel that something odd and unpleasant has just
happened...and is likely to happen again."

BOB

You're putting us on, right, Violet? Or, could it be our hosts
are putting on a show for us?

VIOLET

Not at all!

HARRY

Don't look at me. Come on, let's play another round.

(MUSIC)

JACKSON

"This time I am *Smee*. I'm terrible at playing games. I don't get very far before Violet finds me. Soon everyone finds us and the game is over. We return to the sitting-room for another round of *Smee*. For some reason…I have a feeling that nobody is really enjoying the game any more. But everyone is too polite to mention it. All the same, something feels wrong. All the fun has gone out of the game. Something deep inside me is trying to warn me. `Take care,' it whispers. `Take care'. Can there be some unnatural, unhealthy influence at work in the house? Why do I have this feeling? Because Harry had counted thirteen people instead of twelve? I'm sure he wasn't fooling us. Anyway, I'd like to laugh, but, I can't.

(WHISTLE)

"Well, we start again. While we're all chasing the unknown `Smee' we are all as noisy as ever. But it seems to me that most of us are just acting. We are no longer enjoying the game. At first I stay with the others. But for several minutes no `Smee' is found. I leave the main group and start searching on the first floor at the west side of the house. And there, while I am feeling my way along, I bump into a pair of human knees. I put out my hand and touch a soft, heavy curtain. I know where I am. There are tall, deep windows with window-seats at the end of the corridor. The curtains reach to the ground. Somebody is sitting in a corner of one of the window-seats, behind a curtain. So, I think I've caught *Smee.* I yank the curtain to one side …

(CURTAIN SWISH)

"and suddenly touch a woman's arm. Through the frosted window I can see that it's a dark, moonless night outside. I can't see the woman sitting in the corner of the window-seat." *Smee?* "No answer. Well, I've lost the challenge. So I sit down beside her to wait for the others. Then I whisper," What's your name? "And out of the darkness beside me the whisper comes..."

WOMAN'S VOICE

Brenda Ford.

JACKSON

"Hmm, I don't know the name... but I guess at once who she is. I know every girl in the house by name... except one. It's the tall, pale, dark girl. So, here she is sitting beside me on the window-seat, shut in between a heavy curtain and a window. Well, I'm beginning to enjoy this game. I wonder if she is enjoying it too." So, Brenda... here we are, alone...in the dark...? Do you come here often? "No answer." Alright, I know, this is a game of silence. We have to be quiet. But, there's nobody else about. Let's break a few rules. Starting with a pleasant conversation...even if we have to whisper. Well? "No answer. I'm beginning to feel a little annoyed. Perhaps, she is one of those cold, clever girls who have a poor opinion of all men. She doesn't like me, and she is using the rules of the game as an excuse for not speaking. Alright, if she doesn't like sitting here with me, I certainly don't want to sit with her! I hope someone finds us...and soon! I thought that the girl I had seen at dinner might be likeable, even if in a cold kind of way. I had certainly wanted to know more about her. But, now I feel really uncomfortable beside her. She's so still. I don't even hear her breathing. My heart is starting to beat real fast. Faster. I reach out and touch her arm...what? I'm trembling with horror. I want to jump up and run away. Please! Somebody, come and find us! Who's there? Someone is coming! Oh, thank the Lord! "

(CURTAIN SWISH)

VIOLET

Smee?

JACKSON

"It's Violet! Of course she receives no answer. So, she sits down beside me, and at once I feel very much better. She whispers..."

VIOLET

It's Jackson, isn't it?

JACKSON

Yes.

VIOLET

You're not *Smee*, are you?

JACKSON

No, she's on my other side.

VIOLET

Hello, *Smee*. How are you? Who are you?

JACKSON

You're breaking the rules, Violet. And this one here, she certainly plays by the rules.

VIOLET

Oh, who cares about the rules? I'm fed up with this game anyway. I hope they aren't going to play it all evening. I'd like to play a nice quiet game, all together beside a warm fire.

JACKSON

Me too.

VIOLET

Maybe we can change their minds.

JACKSON

It's Harry. He's the instigator.

VIOLET

I'm sure I'm being very silly. But I can't get rid of the idea that we've got an extra player . . . somebody who ought not to be here at all.

JACKSON

That is exactly how I feel.

VIOLET

You too? I wonder when the others will find us? Oh, I hear them coming now...

(CURTAIN SWISH)

HARRY

Hello, hello! Is anybody there?

JACKSON

Yes.

HARRY

Is Violet with you?

JACKSON

Yes.

HARRY

What happened to you? You are both the losers in this round.
We've all been waiting for you for hours.

JACKSON

But, you haven't found *Smee* yet.

HARRY

You haven't, you mean. I was *Smee* this time.

JACKSON

That's ridiculous! *Smee* is here with us!

VIOLET

Yes! She's right over...here...?

JACKSON

"I look at Violet and she at me and then we look to her other
side and...there is an empty place on the window seat."

HARRY

Oh, really?

JACKSON

But...

VIOLET

This is too strange. I think I'm going to be sick.

JACKSON

There was somebody there! I touched her.

VIOLET

So did I. And, I don't think anyone could leave this window-seat without us knowing.

HARRY

Yeah, right! Someone's been playing jokes on all of us tonight. Are you coming down?

(MUSIC)

Here they are, folks. I found the two of them sitting behind a curtain, on a window-seat.

JACKSON

"I go straight up to the tall, dark girl." So you pretended to be *Smee*, and then went away! "She gives me a dirty look, shakes her head, as if I'm insane. Afterwards, we all play cards in the sitting-room. I'm more relaxed now. But...there's something amiss...Harry has been acting strangely. Finally, he calls me into the next room..."

HARRY

Look, Jackson...I may have had a few too many whiskey sours tonight... but, I know what I know...can see with my own eyes...and if you're in love with my wife, Violet ...you'd better come right out and say it...because what you two did tonight...hiding behind that curtain, the two of you...for all that time...keeping us all waiting...it was very rude of you, my own cousin...I'm ashamed of you.

JACKSON

But, Harry, you have to believe me! Believe Violet! We were not alone! There was somebody else there ...somebody who was pretending to be *Smee*. I believe it was that tall, dark girl, that Miss Ford. She even whispered her name to me. Of course, she refused to admit it afterwards.

HARRY

Miss *who?*

JACKSON
Brenda Ford…that's what she said her name is.

HARRY
Look here, Jackson…I don't mind a joke, but enough is enough. We don't want to worry the ladies and create a disturbance here tonight. It's Christmas Eve.

JACKSON
What are you talking about?

HARRY
Brenda Ford? Brenda Ford is the name of the girl who broke her neck on the stairs…the one who was playing hide and seek here ten years ago. So, if you're playing me for the fool…

_____

THE SPECTRE BRIDEGROOM
By Dan Bianchi
From A Story By William Hunt

Cast - 3m, 2w
Running Time - 14 min
Synopsis - A man returns from the dead to the girl he loves

(MUSIC)

NARRATOR
There's this wealthy ship builder named Lenine... lives in
Gloucester. He has but one son, Frank Lenine, a wayward lad.
So, his parents indulge him in all his faults... particularly, his
dalliances with the servant girls. There is one, a young girl,
Nancy Trenoweth, who especially assists Mrs. Lenine in all the
various duties the house. Nancy...she's very pretty, but,
uneducated, yet, she's not stupid by any means. She
possesses a certain grace, but, knows nothing of the world
outside a fishing village. Poor girl, she's a dreamer, and so,
she's open to influences. For instance, her mother...

MRS.TRENOWETH
Nancy, you hold your head up high, girl. Haven't I taught you
that everything in nature is home to some spirit? We
Trenoweths are not like the rest of these servants. We work for
our living, true, but, we do not believe we are inferior to our
employers. Remember that.

NARRATOR
In the Lenine house, Nancy spends a great deal of time with her
mistress, until they become very close and she's almost
regarded as a daughter. Unfortunately, that means she spend
a good deal of time around young Frank Lenine... who is
regarded as the handsomest young man in the parish. Well, it
isn't long before Frank and Nancy....

FRANK
Come here and give me a kiss, girl...

NANCY
I'm not your girl...

FRANK

Oh, yes you are.

NANCY

But, what if your parents find out?

FRANK

And, what if they did? They think the sun rises and sets on me.
I can do anything I want. Anyway, though they're blind to it,
the whole parish knows about us. Tomorrow ...tomorrow I will
tell them and...

NANCY

And?

FRANK

And, I will ask for their consent to marry you.

NARRATOR

So, the next morning, he asks...

MR. LENINE

Are you out of your mind? Just because we have allowed you
all sorts of things, our only son...since you were a tot...having
your own way...but, this, *this* is different. This is an outrage!
A disgrace! She's not one of us. Marry a servant girl? And to
carry on behind our backs...? That's the thanks we get for
bringing her into our house? You can forget any ideas of
marriage, boy...I want this sordid relationship to end this
minute. She's going home to her parents and you're never to
see her again. Is that clear?

FRANK

But, Father...

MR.LENINE

If you dare to see her again, you'll be cut off from the Lenine
name and all that goes with it...that's my solemn word.

NARRATOR

The commands of the old are generally powerless upon the
young where the affairs of the heart are concerned. Frank,

who is usually home every evening with his folks, is now gone each night. The once happy household has become gloomy. Parents and son rarely speak to one another. If they do talk, it turns into bitter arguments, especially if they dare ask him about his nightly wanderings.

NANCY
Oh, Frank, you're going to be disowned by your father if he should ever find us together.

FRANK
Let him! What do I care? Who do they think they are, telling me what to do? Anyway, let's not talk about them. Here...I brought you my lock of hair as you had asked. Do you have one for me?

NANCY
Yes. Oh, yes.

FRANK
Lovely. And...here it is...

NANCY
The ring? But, where did you get it?

FRANK
I did as you said. I got it from the finger of a corpse. You should have seen me last night in the churchyard, digging up old Mr.Frawley, like some grave robbing ghoul.

NANCY
They say that a vow taken with such a ring will never be broken. Forever we will be united, either dead or alive.

FRANK
You and your spiritualism.

NANCY
Look at the moon, Frank, so big and round and smiling down on us. Let's swear our love, Frank, together, forever, under the moon.

NARRATOR
Time passes and no matter how hard the lovers try to keep their nightly trysts a secret…it soon becomes evident to Nancy's parents that she is with child.

MRS.TRENOWETH
Well, Mr.Lenine, what shall we do about this now? My daughter did not get in this way by herself, you know? It's only right that your boy marry my Nancy.

MR.LENINE
That will never happen.

NARRATOR
Mr.Lenine has other plans. He takes his son away to Plymouth…where, despite all protests…the boy succumbs to his father's persuasion and brow beating punishment and signs on to work aboard a ship bound for India. It's all happened so quickly, Frank can't write to Nancy…and when he does, her own parents make sure that she never receives his letters. A few months later…
(CHILDBIRTH, BABY CRIES)

A babe is born into a troublesome world… and the infant becomes a real solace to the young mother. As the child grows, Nancy eventually forgets her sorrow, but, never her lover…

NANCY
Frank, wherever you be…I am present with you, remember that in your hour of temptation. No distance can separate our souls…no time can be long enough to destroy the bond between us.

NARRATOR
Well, times are hard and Nancy, once again, finds herself working as a maid while her mother raises the child. Like her mother before her, Nancy carries an air of superiority amongst the other servants. The younger girls swarm about her as if she is a woman of the world. She tells them tales filled with superstitions of the time and place. Still, she can never forget.

NANCY

It's been three years since Frank left the country. Not a word from him since then. I'm told his own parents have not heard from him. Sure, now they want to see his child. To become its grandparents. They've even invited me to come and live with them. Ha!

NARRATOR

One night, All-Hallows' eve, two of Nancy's companions persuade her to go with them and sow hemp-seed in the hope that they'll each find their true love. At midnight the three girls trot out to the field to perform their incantation. Nancy is the first to sow, scattering the seed...and reciting three times...

NANCY

Hemp-seed I sow thee, Hemp-seed grow thee...and he who will my true love be, come after me and show thee. Hemp-seed I sow thee, Hemp-seed grow thee...and he who will my true love be, come after me and show thee...Hemp-seed I sow thee, Hemp-seed grow thee...and he who will my true love be, come after me And show thee.

NARRATOR

Now, just as she finishes that last line, she looks back over her left shoulder and whom should she see?

NANCY

Frank! He's coming this way. It's him...it's him.... But...but, he looks so angry! (Screams)

NARRATOR

Her terror breaks the spell. Well, as you can imagine...the girls are a bit shaken by this, but, that doesn't stop Charlotte who is resolved to find herself a husband. But, when she recites the incantation three times...

(SCREAMS)

What has she seen? A white coffin. Fear now takes hold and all leave the field in a hurry to their homes...where each spend a sleepless night.

(THUNDER)

November arrives and with it...a terrific storm that drives a large ship into the rocks just north of Gloucester.... where it lies beaten by the impetuous waves and is soon in pieces. Amongst the bodies of the crew washed ashore, nearly all of whom had perished, is Frank Lenine. But, he's not dead, yet.

FRANK

Send for...Nancy Trenoweth...please! Send for Nancy! I beg you! I must make her my wife before I...

NARRATOR

Frank is taken home, but, dies before he reaches the front door. His parents, overwhelmed in their own sorrows, think nothing of Nancy, and without her knowing that Frank has returned, the poor fellow Is laid in his last bed, in St.Bernard's Churchyard. Elsewhere...On the night of the funeral, Nancy makes her rounds of the house where she is employed, locking the doors and windows. She stops to look out the window into the night and she hears....

(HORSE APPROACHING)

NANCY

What's that? A horse...a rider is coming. Riding like the devil. He's stopping out by the road...he's looking this way...

NARRATOR

But, it's too dark out there. She throws up the window to get a better view and at that instant, her blood runs cold...

NANCY

That horse...I know that horse...it's Frank's colt...but, I can't see the rider in the shadows...

FRANK (ECHO)

Nancy!

NANCY

Frank...?

NARRATOR

She's near fainting. Can it be? The figure upon the horse...looks very sorrowful, and deathly pale...

NANCY

Frank? Is that you?

FRANK (ECHO)

I have just arrived home...I've come to make you my bride.
Come and join me, my dearest love...hurry, we must be married
before morning.

NARRATOR

Naturally, Nancy is excited by the news. In a few seconds, she
is outside and springing up behind him upon his horse...but,
when she takes his hand, a shiver passes through her...

NANCY

It's cold as ice.

NARRATOR

And as she grasps his waist to secure herself in her seat, her
arm becomes as stiff as ice and she loses all power of speech.

NANCY

I'm frightened, but I don't know why.
                                        (WIND, GALLOPING HORSE)

NARRATOR

The moon has arisen, and now bursts out in a full flood of light,
through the heavy clouds which have obscured it. The horse
flies through the night and if it should slow down but a bit, its
rider drives it on. Beyond this, no word has been spoken since
Nancy mounted the horse behind her lover. They now come to
Trove's Crossing and dash through the river. The moon shines
full in their faces. Nancy looks into the stream, and finally sees
a clear reflection of her lover...

NANCY

A shroud...he's wearing a shroud...the clothing of the grave!
Now I know! I'm being carried away by a spirit!

NARRATOR

Yet, she has no power to save herself.

NANCY

I'm helpless. Can't move! Can't free myself.

NARRATOR

On they go, riding at a furious pace...until they come to the blacksmith's shop...and she can see by the light from the forge fire thrown across the road that the smith is still at work.   She now recovers speech.

NANCY

Save me! Save me! Save me!

NARRATOR

The smith springs out from the barn doors with a red-hot iron in his hand, and as the horse rushes by, he catches the woman's dress, and pulls her to the ground. The spirit, however, also seizes Nancy's dress with one hand in a viselike grip.

FRANK (ECHO)

Where do you think *you're* going?

NARRATOR

The horse passes like the wind, and Nancy and the smith are pulled down the road as far as the churchyard. Here the horse for a moment stops. The smith seizes that moment, and with his hot iron burns off the dress from the rider's hand, thus saving Nancy, more dead than alive... while the rider passes over the wall of the churchyard, and vanishes on the grave in which Frank Lenine had been laid but a few hours before. Well, the neighbors take poor Nancy back to her parents and she is put to bed.

NANCY

Please...let me see my daughter. Mother...I want...you must...

MRS.TRENOWETH

Shush, now, rest...

NANCY

No...I want you to give her to Frank's parents...to raise. And...and...I want to be buried in Frank's grave. Promise me...

MRS.TRENOWETH
Don't say such things, child...

NARRATOR
But, by morning, Nancy has taken her last breath. That night...Frank's colt is seen barreling as fast as a bullet through the streets and is later found...dead, covered with foam, its eyes forced from its head, and its swollen tongue hanging out of its mouth. On Frank Lenine's grave is discovered the piece of Nancy's dress which was left in the spirit's hand when the blacksmith freed her from his grasp. A day later, at the funeral...a sailor who had survived the shipwreck comes forth to tell the Lenines...

SAILOR
It was on the 30th of October, at night, All Hallows Eve, right? All of a sudden, Frank Lenine, your son, he's like a mad man, he is. We can scarcely keep him in the ship. He seems more asleep than awake, and, after great excitement, he falls down as if dead upon the deck, and lays that way for hours. When he comes to...he tells us a strange thing. Says he had been taken to this here very village...well, that is, his spirit was suddenly taken, to right here...and mad as hell he is about it. Angry? You should have seen his face. Swears that if he should ever marry the woman who has cast the spell, he will make her suffer the longest day she has to live... for drawing his soul out of his body like that.

NARRATOR
Poor Nancy is granted her request to be buried in Frank Lenine's grave...and as for her friend Charlotte who had also sowed the hemp-seed and had seen the white coffin...within a month, she's sleeping beside her.

THE MUSIC ON THE HILL
By Dan Bianchi
From A Story By Saki

Cast - 2m, 1w
Running Time - 14 min
Synopsis - A woman moves to the country and encounters
ghostly music

(MUSIC)

NARRATOR

Sylvia Seltoun ate her breakfast with a pleasant sense of
ultimate victory. She was not a born fighter, but, fate had
thrown her a series of small struggles, usually with the odds
slightly against her, and usually she had just managed to come
out on top. Today, she felt as if she had won her hardest
battle yet. To have married Malcolm Seltoun was step one.
She knew she'd have to face the cold hostility of his family.
That required her determination and skillfulness. Yesterday
she had brought her victory to its concluding stage by
wrenching her stuffed-shirt, businessman of a husband away
from his mother and settling him down in the country. She
could still hear Mrs.Seltoun...

SYLVIA

Telling me that I'll never get her son to leave. "He belongs here
with us," she said. "He's a city boy," she said. She doesn't
want us settling all the way out there in Yessney. "I doubt that
will ever happen," she said. Ha!

NARRATOR

It's true, Sylvia was not born and bred in the country, herself.
But, she learned to appreciate its wholesomeness. The pure
air and clean living was good for a person. She had hoped to
take many long walks in the woods. Maybe, even with
Malcolm. She was happy that her will-power and strategy had
prevailed. He would stay. He would never go back to mother.
She looked outside to her lawn. A lawn. She'd never had a
lawn before today. And hedges. And a steep slope of heather.
There's an oak tree and a yew. All new to her and somewhat
mysterious, too. Wild, savage.

SYLVIA

Malcolm...you know, it is very wild out here. Exciting, don't you think? Listen to the forest. It's alive, but, also lonely.

MALCOLM

What are you going on about?

SYLVIA

I mean, one might even suppose that in such a place ...there are those who still worship the ancient pagan gods. I found a statue on a pedestal out there in a clearing. A statue of Pan.

MALCOLM

Who?

SYLVIA

Pan. The Nature-God. You know, he has horns on his head and he's half goat and has hooves, I think. Most of his children were stillborn.

MALCOLM

Really? And, you know this as a fact?

SYLVIA

Haven't you ever heard of Pan?

MALCOLM

The only Pan I know is Peter...and only by name.

NARRATOR

A week later, Sylvia had exhausted the attractions of the woodland walks around Yessney. Then, she ventured on a tour of inspection of the farm buildings. A farmyard suggested in her mind a scene of cheerful bustle, with churns and smiling dairymaids, and teams of horses drinking knee-deep in duck-crowded ponds. As she wandered among the gaunt grey buildings of Yessney manor farm her first impression was one of crushing stillness and desolation. It was lonely here. Something seemed to give her a sinister feeling about the place. She could hear the life behind the walls...but nothing to be seen.

(OWL HOOT, HORSE SNORT, HOOF STAMP,

CHAIN RATTLE, COW MOO,
CHICKENS, DOG, GATE OPEN)

Sylvia felt that if she had come across any human beings in
this wilderness they would have fled like ghosts. At last,
turning a corner quickly, she did come upon a living thing.
Stretched out in a pool of mud was an enormous sow, who
didn't care to be interrupted.

(PIG SQUEAL)

Sylvia retreated, threading her way past fences and cowsheds
and long blank walls. And then she heard...

(BOY LAUGHS)

Joseph, the only boy employed on the farm was visibly at work
on a potato patch half-way up the nearest hill-side.
As the days passed, she saw very little of her husband.
Malcolm loved to go fishing in nearby streams. One day, she
followed him...but, lost her way and soon found herself in a
familiar clearing surrounded by huge yew trees. In the middle
of the clearing there stood a stone pedestal on top of which
stood a small bronze figure of a youthful Pan.

SYLVIA
Now, how did I get here? Well, look at that...

NARRATOR
It was a beautiful piece of workmanship. But, that's not what
had caught her attention. No, because, at its feet was an
offering of a freshly cut bunch of grapes.

SYLVIA
Grapes? Where did these come from?

NARRATOR
Grapes were a luxury around here. She knew that there weren't
any to be found at the manor house. What were they doing out
here? She snatched them from the pedestal. There was
something about this that made her angry...and a bit afraid,
too. As she walked back to the house... she suddenly
saw...there, across a thick tangle of undergrowth a boy's face
was scowling at her, beautiful and tanned, with unutterably evil

eyes. She sped forward without waiting to give a closer look to this sudden apparition. When she had reached the main path, she realized she had dropped the grapes along the way.

(MUSIC)

SYLVIA
I saw a young boy in the woods today. He was quite tan. Rather handsome. But, he was off in the bushes, hiding from me.

MALCOLM
Was it the boy who works on the farm?

SYLVIA
No...I don't...no. Are there any gypsies around here?

MALCOLM
Nope. No gypsies.

SYLVIA
Then who was he?

MALCOLM
I have no idea.

SYLVIA
I suppose it was your doing? The grapes? There were grapes on the statue of Pan. I saw it.

MALCOLM
Nope, not me. Did you...fool with it in any way?

SYLVIA
What? No, I threw the grapes away. Silly. What, is it some sort of local native custom or something?

MALCOLM
I don't think you were wise to do that. Maybe the Wood Gods are rather horrible to those who molest them.

SYLVIA
Horrible, perhaps, to those that believe in them, but, you see, I

don't.

MALCOLM

You're the one who wanted to know about Pan. All the same, I should avoid the woods and orchards if I were you, and beware of the horned beasts on the farm.

SYLVIA

Now you're making fun of me.

MALCOLM

I'm not the one imagining things. I'm having a fine time catching trout.

SYLVIA

That's all you ever do. Trout.

MALCOLM

I'm enjoying the country. That's what you wanted, isn't it?

SYLVIA

Yes, but...I mean...we can go back to the city for awhile, if you like?

NARRATOR

Her victory had not been so complete as she had supposed. She was surprised to find that she was already anxious to quit country life altogether.

MALCOLM

Mother said you'd have us running back to town in a week or so.

SYLVIA

Nevermind. We're staying.

NARRATOR

She'd just avoid going into the woods. Which didn't leave much for her to do. There were the cows. The rams. The orchard. Each day, the same thing. Life in the country was boring.

(FLUTE)

SYLVIA

What...is that?

(RESTLESS ANIMALS, SNORTS)

NARRATOR

Sylvia turned her steps in an upward direction and climbed the slopes that stretched high above Yessney. There was something in the wind. It was leading her away from the farm.

(DISTANT HOUNDS HUNTING)

From high up, she looked down across the meadow and there were the hounds in full chase. A deer was leaping in and out of the forest.

SYLVIA

The poor thing!

NARRATOR

At last he broke through the outermost line of oak scrub and fern and stood panting in the open, a fat September stag carrying a full rack of antlers.

SYLVIA

He's heading toward the sea. He'll be trapped.

NARRATOR

To Sylvia's surprise, however, he turned his head to the upland slope.

SYLVIA

This is terrible. He's out in the open. The hounds will get him. They'll tear him apart.

NARRATOR

But, then, the noise of the pack seemed to die away and in its place...

(FLUTE)

Sylvia stood half hidden in a thick growth of bushes, and watched the wild stag swing upward, toward her. The pipe music shrilled suddenly around her, seeming to come from the bushes at her very feet, and at the same moment the great beast turned round and bore directly down upon her. In an instant her pity for the hunted animal was changed to wild terror! She wanted to flee, but, found herself tangled in the thick heather beneath her feet. The hounds were getting closer. But, closer still was that giant stag with its huge antlers, those spikes were but a few yards from her...

MALCOLM

(ECHO) Beware of the horned beasts....

NARRATOR

And then with a quick throb of joy she saw that she was not alone....a human figure stood a few paces aside, knee-deep in the bushes.

SYLVIA

Drive it off! Drive it away!

NARRATOR

But, the figure made no answering movement. The antlers drove straight at her breast, the acrid smell of the hunted animal was in her nostrils....but, her eyes were filled with the horror of something she saw other than her oncoming death. And in her ears rang the echo of....

(BOY LAUGHING)

A GHOST
By Dan Bianchi
From A Story By Guy De Maupassant

Cast - 3m,1w
Running Time - 14 min
Synopsis - A man encounters a female ghost

(MUSIC)

NARRATOR
"Something strange happened to me ten years ago. It's haunted me every day. It's filled me with such a deep, mysterious unrest that, all these years, I've kept it to myself. Kept it hidden, like a sad, shameful secret. Now, I must confess it. So, here it is…just as it took place. Just don't ask me to explain it.

(MUSIC)

"July, 1917, I am living in an apartment on lower Fifth Avenue. One day, as I'm strolling in Washington Square, I come across a man I believe I've seen before. I can't place him with certainty. Instinctively, I walk slower. The stranger looks at me and nearly falls into my arms. Well, he's a friend from my younger days! Now, he looks twice his age, thoroughly exhausted. Quite drunk." Gabriel Parsons, what's happened to you, my friend?

GABRIEL
A terrible thing… has broken me, completely.

NARRATOR
"And so, the liquor in him begins to tell me of the events which have led to his current situation."

GABRIEL
Some time ago, I had fallen madly in love with a young girl…I married her. Life was a dream. We lived out in the countryside. For a whole year, sheer bliss. Then, she died suddenly of heart disease…

NARRATOR

Oh, I'm sorry.

GABRIEL

I think love itself killed her. So, I left the countryside on the
very day of her funeral. I live here now, in the hotel. I lead a
solitary life...desperate. My grief is slowly eating away at me. I
must admit...I've thought of leaping off the The Brooklyn
Bridge more than once. But, now, my friend, now that I've
come across you again....I shall ask a great favor of you.

NARRATOR

Anything.

GABRIEL

I want you to go to my house where I had lived with her ...and
retrieve some papers I urgently need. They are in the writing-
desk of my room, of *our* room. I cannot send a servant or a
lawyer, as the errand must be kept private. I want absolute
silence. I'll give you the key to the room, which I locked
carefully myself before leaving... and the key to the writing-
desk. I shall also give you a note for the caretaker, who will let
you in.

NARRATOR

I can do that.

GABRIEL

Come to breakfast with me tomorrow, and we'll talk the matter
over.

NARRATOR

That's easy enough. But, your home is twenty five miles out in
the country.

GABRIEL

Take my automobile. You can be there in an hour's time.

(MUSIC)

NARRATOR

"At ten o'clock the next day, we have breakfast, but he barely
talks at all."

GABRIEL

You must excuse me for my silence. You see, just the thought of you visiting the very house that was once filled with my joy is upsetting. Now, let me explain exactly what you must do. It's simple. Take two packages of letters and some papers, locked in the first drawer at the right of the desk...you have the key. Please do not read these papers.

NARRATOR

Of course not.

GABRIEL

Forgive me, I didn't wish to imply...It hurts me so much...

NARRATOR

"As tears come to his eyes, I bid him farewell."

GABRIEL

Good luck, my friend. And thank you.

(MUSIC, CAR)

NARRATOR

"It's a beautiful day, the drive is pleasant. The paved road turns to dirt as I enter the forest...a bit more treacherous where it has turned to mud. I've noticed that the note to the caretaker is sealed. Why would he do that? Doesn't he trust me? On the other hand, perhaps, it was just an oversight on his part. He was rather upset by it all. There's his house. Looks as though it's been deserted for years. The gate, wide-open and rotten. Barely holding on to its hinges. The driveway is grown over with grass and weeds. There's an old man. Must be the caretaker."

(CAR SHUTS OFF. DOOR SLAM)

Hello! I've got a letter for you.

CARETAKER

Well, what do you want?

NARRATOR

Read it. The owner of this place wants me to be allowed into the house. I have to get something.

CARETAKER

(Pause) So...you're going in...his room?

NARRATOR

Why do you care?

CARETAKER

Well, it's just...it has not been opened since...since the death. If you will wait five minutes, I will go in to see whether...

NARRATOR

There's nothing to see. Besides, I have the key to the room.

CARETAKER

Oh? Oh, alright, follow me.

NARRATOR

Show me the stairs and leave me alone. I can find it without your help.

CARETAKER

Still....I....

NARRATOR

Don't worry yourself. I'll do it myself. "I find my way through the house to the main staircase and go upstairs. The door is to the right...

(UNLOCK, DOOR OPEN)

"Dark in here. Can't see a thing. And, it's moldy and stale. Phew! A dead odor. Now, from the hall light, I can just see a bed without sheets having still its mattresses and pillows... one bears a deep print of an elbow or a head, as if someone has just been resting on it. A few chairs here and there. The closet door looks open. I'll just throw open the shade to let in some light.

(OPENS SHADES)

"Ah, the outside wooden shutters are rusted shut...no, they won't budge open. I'm feeling irritated...the long drive, that caretaker...let's just hurry and get this over with. At least, my eyes are adjusting to the dim light. Aha! There's the desk drawer I'm looking for.

(OPENS LOCK)

"Full to the brim. I am looking for three packages. Come on, where are they?

(RUSTLING NOISE)

"What's that? Nothing. Probably the shade. Pay no attention. Keep looking for the packages. Here's one...ah, here's another...

(DEEP SIGH)

"Alright, I heard that. Someone is here with me...Oh my God! It's a woman...a tall woman, dressed in white ....facing me, standing behind the chair. But, this is ridiculous. It can't be. Look at me, I'm trembling! It's as if my whole body is limp as a sponge....I'm collapsing inside. No, I don't believe in ghosts. But, that can't be a real woman. A dead woman. Is that why I am shaking like a leaf in a hurricane? If she speaks, I'll die. Right here and now."

WOMAN
Oh, you can be of great help to me...

NARRATOR
"I try to answer, but I'm unable to utter one word."

WOMAN
Will you? You can save me, cure me. I suffer terribly. I always suffer. I suffer, oh, I suffer! Will you?

NARRATOR
"I nod my head, being still paralyzed. She hands me a woman's comb of tortoise-shell."

WOMAN
Comb my hair! Please, comb my hair! That will cure me. Look at my head...how I suffer! And my hair...how it hurts!

NARRATOR
"Her loose hair, very long, very black, hangs over the back of the chair, touching the floor. Why do I do it? Why do I,

shivering with fear... accept that comb, and why do I take between my hands her long hair, which leaves on my skin a ghastly impression of cold? It's as if I am handling cold, slimy, wriggling eels. I don't know. That feeling still clings about my fingers, and I shiver when I recall it. Yet, I comb her hair. Don't ask me how. It seems to make her happy."

WOMAN
Thank you!

NARRATOR
"Oh! Where has she gone? She's ripped the comb from my hand and fled through the door. What was that all about? A nightmare? Pull yourself together. I run to the window and break those shutters...

(WOOD SPLINTERS)

"... and a stream of light pours in. The door! The door where she has disappeared behind...

(RATTLES DOORKNOB)

"Locked. Get out of here! Get out now! Panic overtakes me. Grab those three packages and run. Out of the room. Down the staircase, three steps at a time. Out the front door and into my car.

(CAR STARTS, TAKES OFF)

"I drive away and don't stop until I am home.

(MUSIC)

"For the past hour, I've been asking myself if I've not been hallucinating. I've seen something, certainly. Look at me, I'm a nervous wreck. No, there's nothing supernatural about it. There's a perfectly logical explanation. An optical illusion? Oh my God! Look at this...and this! My jacket is covered with hairs, long hairs...a woman's hairs...

(MUSIC)

"I need to think this over. What am I going to tell my friend? I sent his letters to him. He received them. He called, but, my servant told him that I am sick. I'm told he's very upset. But, now, a week later... I am upset...you see, I went to see him, yesterday, finally…I wanted to tell him the truth. But, he's not there. He hasn't been seen all week. I notified the police. They search for him everywhere, but no one can find any trace of him. They've even searched his house in the country. No suspicious clue has been discovered.   There is no sign that a woman has been concealed there. The investigation yields nothing, and so the search goes no further.

(MUSIC)

"Years have passed…about my friend's disappearance, I have learned nothing more. Where did he go? What was in those three letters? I never did find out the truth."

OUT OF THE SEA
By Dan Bianchi
From A Story By A.C. Benson

Cast - 3m, 1w
Running Time - 20 min
Synopsis - An invisible being seeks revenge against a
murderer

(MUSIC, SEA GULLS)

NARRATOR
Hampden is a little village on the sea...about thirty houses, it
was once a thriving port, but, now very poor. Mostly
fishermen. It's a desolate place. Cut off from the world. The
church, built in better days, has a roof that's nearly gone at one
end and five or six windows missing altogether. When the
wind blows, and it does pretty steadily...it whistles so loudly
through the open church ...it can be heard for a good mile or
so. But, what can be done? Father Thomas is helpless. He
lives in an ancient brick house nearby. Raises herbs. A kind
man, but, getting on in years. It's a quiet life amongst his small
flock.

THOMAS
There's a chill in the wind, today. Ah, here comes visitors...

NARRATOR
Three of them... John Grimston, the richest man in the place,
half farmer and half fisherman, a dark surly old man... his wife,
Bridget, a timid and frightened woman, who found life with her
harsh husband a difficult business, in spite of their
wealth...and their son Henry, a silly shambling man of forty.
His father regards him as the town misfit.

THOMAS
Hello! And what may I do for you?

BRIDGET
We have a matter, Father, we would ask you about...are you at
leisure?

THOMAS

I am ashamed to be not more busy! Let's go within the house.

NARRATOR

His visitors act strangely, subdued, yet, peering over their shoulders often and around his house, as if they are being followed, or watched. Once inside the parlor, they sit quietly glancing at each other. Father Thomas doesn't know what to make of it all...this is an odd way to act for the Grimston family.

JOHN

Come, wife, tell the tale and make an end of it. We must not take up the Father's time.

BRIDGET

I hardly know how to say it, Father...but a strange and evil thing has befallen us... there is something come to our house, and we know not what it is...but, it brings a fear with it.

NARRATOR

The poor woman looks deathly pale, visibly terrified. She can hardly speak.

HENRY

It is an evil beast out of the sea.

NARRATOR

A dreadful silence follows. Now, Father Thomas is naturally a cheerful fellow...he needs to muster some of that cheerfulness and rescue the situation somewhat.

THOMAS

Sea beasts? Come, come...must we talk about such things? On a lovely day such as this?

NARRATOR

They say nothing.

THOMAS

Well...if we must...why not begin at the beginning, Mrs.Grimston? But, don't be afraid, now, nothing can touch us here.

BRIDGET

It was the day of the ship wreck, Father. John and Henry walked out early to the beach, they were the first to see the ship wreck. John told me there was a wreck ashore, and they went presently and roused the rest of the village…. and all that day they were out, saving what could be saved. Two sailors were found, both dead and pitifully battered by the sea, and they were buried, as you know, Father, in the churchyard next day… John came back about dusk and Henry with him, and we sat down to our supper. John was telling me about the wreck, as we sat beside the fire, when…

(MUSIC)

HENRY

I yelled, "What is that? Something, it ran past me suddenly." That's what I yelled.

THOMAS

Oh? Well, could it have been a dog or cat?

HENRY

It's a beast….a beast about the size of a goat. I never seen anything like it…yet I don't see it clear.   I feel the air blow next to me… and get a whiff of it…phew! it was salt like the sea, but with a kind of dead smell, too.

THOMAS

Was that all you saw? Maybe, you were tired and faint, and the air swam round you suddenly….I've had that happen to me when I'm tired.

HENRY

No, no…this isn't like that…it's a beast, I'm sure of it.

BRIDGET

Well, we have seen it since then. At least I have not seen it clearly, yet, but I have smelt its odor, and it turns me sick…but John and Henry have seen it often…sometimes it lies and seems to sleep, but it watches us… and sometimes, like a dog, it acts friendly, leaping about. John saw it skip upon the sands near the wreck…didn't you, John?

JOHN
Oh shut up, you silly woman. It was not near the wreck, it was out to the East.

THOMAS
Well, that doesn't matter. I've never heard of anything like this. But, I'll come down to your house with a holy book and see if we can't meet this thing head on. I don't know what it is...if it's something that's got its hold on you and your family...or, if there are spirits of evil in the world ...it's written about in the Bible, of course...and the sea, too, doubtless has its monsters...it's a vast place, unexplored and unknown to man...maybe, one of its creatures wandered out of the waves, like a dog that is lost looking for its home. I can't say, till I have met it face to face. But, God gives no power to such things to hurt those who have a fair conscience.

NARRATOR
He stops to look at his brethren before him. Bridget looks hopeful, but, the two men stare at the ground.

THOMAS
Alright, I'll come right now. Let's see if I can cast it out or capture the thing, whatever it is. I am in this place as a soldier of the Lord, to fight with works of darkness. Where's my book? Here now...I'm ready, let's go.
Tell me, has it appeared today?

HENRY
Yes, Father. And, it's in a bad mood. It followed us as though it was angry.

THOMAS
Oh? Well, you speak of this thing as if it's a dog. What's it like?

HENRY
I can never see it clearly. It's like a speck in the eye...It's never there when you look directly at it. It glides away very secretly...but, I think it looks mostly like a goat. Horns. And, hairy. But its eyes...its eyes...they are yellow, like a flame.

THOMAS
John, is this so?

JOHN
Yes, it's true. The thing is a devil and why it's bothering with us, I don't know. But, unless it can be cast out...it will kill me. If it wants money, I've got plenty of it. If you need money, Father...

THOMAS
Let there be no talk of money...although, if I can help you, perhaps, you might want to contribute to church repairs ...as your gratitude to God, of course.

NARRATOR
So, they walk very sadly together through the street. There are few folk about...watching them go by, as solemn as a funeral march. The Grimstons' house is the largest of houses. Walled-in garden, a big strong door, a dark front made of brick.
(DOOR UNLOCKS, CREAKS OPEN)

THOMAS
Well, John, what are you waiting for?

JOHN
You go in first, Father.

THOMAS
Alright...

NARRATOR
Even Father Thomas is beginning to grow fearful of what may lie inside waiting...but, he can't show that fear...

THOMAS
Lock the door behind us, John.
(DOOR LOCK)

NARRATOR
Father Thomas stands in the middle of the parlor where there are chairs gathered around the fireplace. Listening. Listening. It's so calm and quiet, he grows ashamed of his fears.

THOMAS
Now, we will sit here together, and talk as cheerfully as we may, till we have dined. Then, if nothing appears to us...I will go round the house, into every room, and see if we can track the thing to its lair... then, I will stay here until evening prayers...and, then, I will leave and return and lie here tonight. Perhaps, the thing dares not to meet the power of the Church in the day-time... perhaps, it will venture out at night. Maybe, I can communicate with it. So, let's not look so down and defeated. We'll act as if normal.

NARRATOR
So, they sit together and Father Thomas talks of many things, and tells some old legends of saints... and they dine...and, still, nothing appears. After dinner, Father Thomas walks through the house, from room to room and upstairs in the bedrooms, as well. Finally, he comes to the last room, which is locked.

THOMAS
Well, shall we take a look in here?

JOHN
No...there is no need to do that. It leads nowhere... it's just a storage room.

THOMAS
Well, we should look everywhere, John. We can't leave a stone unturned.
(SCRATCHING)

What's that?

JOHN
A rat. Must be a rat got in through a hole to the outside.

NARRATOR
Father Thomas can see by the pale faces of fear staring at him that it is not a rat let loose inside that room.

THOMAS
Come now, John. Where's the key? Open the door.
(DOOR UNLOCKS, CREAKS OPEN)

Well now, what do we have in here? Some boxes, jars, twine and rope. Two wooden chests. A pile of clothes. What's that chest there...looks like water dripping from it...?

JOHN

Nothing, nothing.

THOMAS

Henry! What are you staring at, man?

NARRATOR

Suddenly, Father Thomas turns to look deeply into the shadows of a far corner...and there...in the darkness ...something darker still...shapeless...a sharp smell, as of the sea...mixed with something worse...far worse...there it goes! Past Father Thomas, out the door!

THOMAS

May the Lord God protect us all!

NARRATOR

The frightened family turn to Father Thomas, but, there he stands, fumbling with the book in his hands...reading whatever his eyes fall upon...Hardly knowing what to do or say.

THOMAS

Send forth a legion of angels to protect us, Oh Lord!

NARRATOR

Too late. The thing, whatever it is, is gone. Father Thomas stands dumbfounded. He had not really believed that he would truly encounter anything such as this. Yet, he does believe he has a sacred calling to protect this family from any supernatural thing...from evil itself. The family knows, however, that the priest is shaking, trembling with fright...and that doesn't help to allay their fears, any.

THOMAS

I am afraid, my friends...that what we are facing is a sore affliction of Satan...we must withstand him with good courage and conviction. if there be any mortal sin upon your hearts, see that you confess it and be saved immediately. For as long as a sin lies unrepented, Satan has the power to hurt.

(CHURCH BELL)

I have to return to the church now to say vespers.

BRIDGET

We will go with you, Father.

NARRATOR

There's but a handful of worshippers in the church, which is dark, except for the candle light on Father Thomas. He read the holy service swiftly and courageously, but his face shows concern and dread for what lies ahead.

After vespers, he returns to his house to gather belongings for his night's stay at the Grimstons' house. He locks his front door behind him, walks down the path to the street and...

HENRY

Father! Father!

THOMAS

What is it, Henry? Catch your breath...tell me what's wrong! Here, sit on the bench by the gate. Calm yourself and tell me...

HENRY

Oh Father Thomas...it's terrible. On the day of the ship wreck... my father, he wakes me, you see, early, before dawn and I get dressed and he says there's been a wreck on shore and he grabs a shovel and I'm to come with him, quietly, not to wake my mother...and we go down to the shore and there it is, a big black hulk of a ship lying sideways...in the waves...and first we see a body of a man lying on his face in the sand.

(MUSIC)

JOHN

Is he breathing, Henry?

HENRY

No...he's dead.

(MUSIC)

JOHN

Grab that big bag of his. And, see...in his coat pocket, it's bulging with something. May be valuable.

HENRY

Look! Look around him...see how it glitters.

JOHN

That's gold, boy...

HENRY

Coins.

JOHN

Help me lift the body up...we'll take off his coat. Now, what we have to do, Henry, is to dig a hole in the sand. Then, we'll bury him. Got that?

HENRY

And that's what we did, Father Thomas. We buried the man in the sand. But, then...then...

THOMAS

What, Henry?

(MUSIC)

HENRY

The sand, it's moving and stirring and ...aaahhh!

JOHN

What do you see, man?

HENRY

A hand...it's reaching up and out of the sand...with clutching fingers...

(MUSIC)

JOHN

Henry! There is life in him, yet! Grab that shovel! Keep filling in the sand, boy! Move quickly, don't stop! That's right, up to the top now. More.... more...Now, let's trample over it and smooth it down...that's it. Grab the coat and bag there. Give it to me...here, take the shovel. Let's get out of here. We can't go back through the town. People might be out and about by now. No, we'll have to take the long way back...come on.

(MUSIC)

THOMAS

But why didn't you resist your father, Henry, and save the poor sailor?

HENRY

I dared not. Though I would have done so if I could... but, my father has a power over me, and I must obey him.

THOMAS

This is a serious matter, Henry. But, you have told the story bravely and confessed, so, now, will I absolve you for your sin.

HENRY

Thanks be to God.

THOMAS

Now, have you seen anything...anything that might give reason to why that thing might be connected to the ship wreck?

HENRY

Yes...I have. My father and I have watched it skipping and leaping over the water and over where the man lies buried.

THOMAS

Your father must tell me his story as well...and he must confess to both God and the law of the land.

HENRY

He won't do that.

THOMAS

Then, I will compel him.

HENRY

Please don't tell him I told you, Father...or he will kill me, too.

THOMAS

Have no fear of that. I cannot use your confession to convict another of sin, Henry.

HENRY

I have to get back. If he finds out I am gone...I'm afraid of him, Father. He knows things. He'll know I've been here to confess. I've got to run back now...

NARRATOR

Henry runs off into the descending darkness as dusk covers the small town. Father Thomas makes his way as fast as he can to the Grimstons' house, where Mr.and Mrs.Grimston await him at the gate. Henry stands behind them in the doorway.
(HEAVY DOOR CLOSES)

They have tea in silence and listen for any sound. John Grimston says nothing, never even raising his eyes. He knows Father Thomas is watching. That doesn't stop him from laughing a bit, to himself. Father Thomas sees this ...it causes the blood to freeze in his veins...he wants to accuse John Grimston of murder...but, he contains himself and calls them to pray to God for deliverance and salvation.

THOMAS

Perhaps, Lord God, you may show us in your infinite mercy why this evil has befallen the family of Grimston.

NARRATOR

A short while later, they all go to bed...Henry asks to sleep in the same room as the priest. The house is dark ....silent...
(CLOCK TICKING)

At first, Father Thomas cannot sleep...and neither can Henry...
(SOBBING)

But, at last, the Father drops off into slumber...until..
(CLOCK STRIKES)

THOMAS

What? Who's there?

NARRATOR

Lying there in the dark...there is a sense of horror all about him... and he knows that there is some evil thing lurking near. He surveys the room. Henry mutters in his sleep. Having a bad dream. Do his eyes deceive him? There...by the dying fire in the fireplace, there is something stirring...rising up... as though it had been sleeping there...now awakening, stretching itself. In the dim light, it seems to be playing, posing, as if innocently ...But, how can this be? It's a beast of evil. A dreadful demon. It might even be Satan, himself. No, it grows more vile and wicked by the moment. And, there's that horrible scent again...ugh, foul and disgusting. It turns his stomach. Pray, Thomas, pray! But, no words will come. The evil is too strong for him. Oh dear God...the thing spies Thomas now...and begins to approach the bed...swaying from side to side...glaring at him...coming right up to the bed now...laying its hairy forelegs upon the blanket...those eyes! Those narrow, obscene eyes...burning with a dull yellow light. Staring straight into his soul!

THOMAS
The end is near...I cannot move my hand nor foot...I try and try...

NARRATOR
Try, Thomas, with all your might...fight this evil force...

THOMAS
I will...I will...

NARRATOR
And, in a voice that shocks himself, so loud and screaming, he yells...

THOMAS
God Damn You!

NARRATOR
The beast quivers in rage....but, it drops to the floor and in a moment, it is gone.

HENRY
Father! What's wrong? Is it here?

(DOOR OPENS)

JOHN

What's going on in here?

THOMAS

I'll be alright…light the candle, Henry. Just give me some air…out of my way…I'm going to be sick…

NARRATOR

Father Thomas leaps from the bed and rushes out the door. In the back yard, he vomits and relieves himself and sits and calms down and …

(BRIDGET SCREAMS)

THOMAS

What now?

NARRATOR

He picks himself up and runs back into the house only to find Bridget Grimston bending over her husband who lies on the floor, breathing pitifully…shuddering, trembling. Around the room…chaos…

(NOISE, GLASS BREAKING, FURNITURE CRASHING, WIND)

BRIDGET

Father! Help us!

THOMAS

I'm trying…

NARRATOR

At best, all he can think of is to get down on his knees and pray.

THOMAS

Lord God protect us in our hour of need…God forgive us all…

NARRATOR

Moments later…John Grimston ceases to struggle and lays still.

(SILENCE)

JOHN

Father…Thomas…

THOMAS

John Grimston…the time grows short…give God the Glory and confess your sins before Him…that you may be saved for all eternity…

JOHN

I…I…I killed him…

THOMAS

May the Lord forgive you John Grimston…and may the Heavenly spirit take your soul…amen…

BRIDGET

He's gone…(Sobs)

THOMAS

Come, Henry…help me carry your father to his bed.

NARRATOR

And, they do so…but, Thomas can't help noticing that John's face is badly bruised and battered…as though stamped upon by a hoof of some beast. Father Thomas kneels and prays until the dawn.

(ROOSTER CROWS)

Last night, he learned strange secrets, and something of the dark purposes of God was revealed to him. By ten o'clock, a neighbor arrives to tell him that a body has been found on the shore…covered with sand, strangely enough. A man. Perhaps, a sailor..

THOMAS

We'll bury it along with John Grimston. Bridget… Henry …come here, I'd like to talk to you.

NARRATOR

And, Father Thomas takes them aside. Henry sobs, but, Bridget is very calm.

BRIDGET

Henry has told me everything, Father. We have decided that he

shall do whatever you bid him to do. But, must he be given
over to the law?

THOMAS
No...no. I don't hold Henry accountable for the death of the
man... it was his father's sin...and he's been punished for it.
The secret shall be buried in our hearts. Did you see anything
last night, Bridget?

BRIDGET
No...I awakened to the sound of my husband struggling, as if in
a wrestling match, gasping and grunting...and the room
smelled of that awful odor...And I heard him fall to the floor...

THOMAS
Hmmm...God has shown us significant things...strange things
few have ever witnessed...so, I would say we should all live
humbly forever after and give thanks to God for showing
mercy. Henry...let's go to that store room now.

NARRATOR
He and Henry enter the room...and there in the box that
dripped water... is the coat of the dead man, full of money, and
the bag of money, too. Henry would have cast it back into the
sea. But, the priest says that it should be bestowed plentifully
upon shipwrecked mariners and their heirs. But, the ship was a
foreign ship, and no search ever revealed whence the money
had come, save that it seemed to have been violently come by.
Master Grimston was found to have left much wealth. But,
Bridget would sell the house and the land, and it mostly went
to rebuild the church to God's glory. Then, Bridget and Henry
removed to the vicarage and served Father Thomas faithfully,
and they guarded their secret. And, besides the nave is a little
high turret built, where burns a lamp in a lantern at the top, to
give light to those at sea. Now, as for the beast, he troubled
them no more. But, it is easier to raise up evil than to lay it...
and there are those that say, that, to this day, a man or a
woman with an evil thought in their hearts may see on a certain
evening in November, at the ebb of the tide, a goat-like thing
wade in the water, snuffing at the sand, as though it sought but
found not. But, of this I know nothing.